Gino's Italian Adriatic Escape

A taste of Italy from Veneto to Puglia

Gino D'Acampo

HODDER & STOUGHTON

First published in Great Britain in 2018 by
Hodder & Stoughton
An Hachette UK company

1

A CIP catalogue record for this title is available
from the British Library

Hardback ISBN 978 1 473 69019 6
eBook ISBN 978 1 473 69020 2

Editorial Director: Nicky Ross
Project Editor: Polly Boyd
Design: Georgia Vaux
Photography: Dan Jones
Food Stylists: Lizzie Harris and Rob Allison
Props Stylist: Tonia Shuttleworth
Shoot Producer: Ruth Ferrier
Proofreader: Miren Lopategui
Indexer: Lisa Footitt

Colour origination by Altaimage
Printed and bound Firmengruppe APPL, aprinta
druck, Wemding, Germany

Hodder & Stoughton policy is to use papers that are
natural, renewable and recyclable products and made
from wood grown in sustainable forests. The logging
and manufacturing processes are expected to conform
to the environmental regulations of the country of
origin.

Hodder & Stoughton Ltd
Carmelite House
50 Victoria Embankment
London
EC4Y 0DZ

www.hodder.co.uk

Contents

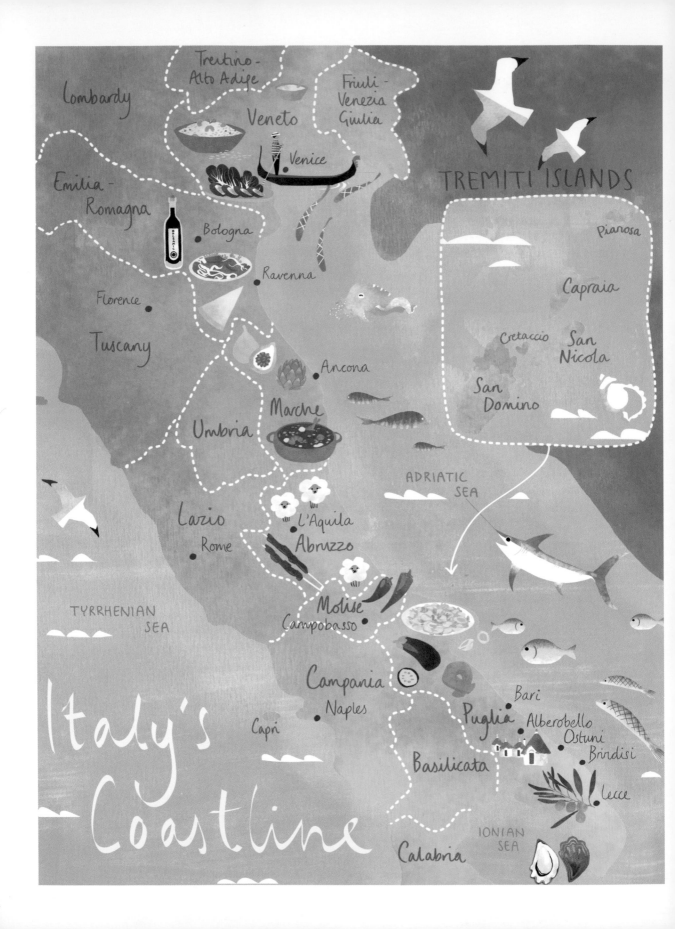

Introduction

I had long wanted to devote a TV series to the sights, culture and *cucina* of Italy's eastern regions. All too often they're overlooked in favour of western Italy, yet there are so many amazing places to visit on the eastern side and the food is incredible. So when I was offered the opportunity to film on the Adriatic coast, I was delighted. From Veneto, in the northeast, all the way down to Puglia, the 'heel' of Italy, this proved to be yet another unforgettable journey through my wonderful homeland.

Venice and Burano

My starting point was Venice, the glorious city built in the middle of the Venetian lagoon and rightly famed as the jewel in the Adriatic crown. Originally constructed on wooden stilts, and believed to be sinking at a rate of 1–2 millimetres each year, it consists of over 100 tiny islands separated by canals and linked by 400 bridges, and is home to more than 450 palaces.

The sights and beauties of Venice are an irresistible lure for visitors from all over the world, but what I particularly enjoyed was getting to know the people who live and work in this magical place. A highlight for me was meeting a fifth-generation gondolier called Riccardo, who told me all about his highly skilled, centuries-old profession. Bearing in mind he's a true Venetian, it was an honour to make him a selection of my favourite *cicchetti* – small, tapas-like snacks that are served with an *aperitivo* in local bars and are a traditional speciality of Venice (see page 12).

Given its history as a wealthy maritime power, and its location on the lagoon, Venice has a long-established and distinctive cuisine that has influenced the region of Veneto as a whole (see pages 26–27). Fish and seafood are a very important part of the Venetian diet, and the Rialto fish market is a must-see for visitors – a centuries-old gem in this vibrant city, it is just the place to enjoy a fresh crab dish with a glass of the local prosecco.

Nearby Burano is also well worth a visit. The island is known for its lace-making traditions and also for its delicious local biscuits called *buranelli*. Traditionally they were prepared by the wives of fishermen for them to take on long fishing expeditions, but are today eaten at celebratory occasions, especially Easter. The houses in Burano are painted a variety of bright colours, and I discovered the reason was so that the fishermen could recognise their own house quickly from the lagoon.

Ravenna and San Marino

So much to see, so much to experience in Veneto – but soon I was on my way south to Ravenna, in the region of Emilia-Romagna (see pages 82–83). The city now lies just inland from the Adriatic but used to be much closer to the sea in ancient times, when it was a notable Roman port. In the 5th century it was the capital of the Roman Empire, and subsequent conquerors left their influences on the city's architecture and art, particularly in the form of many wonderful mosaics. When you're hungry in

Ravenna, the chances are you'll grab a *piadina* – the traditional regional speciality. Essentially an unleavened flatbread, *piadine* are delicious with all kinds of toppings and fillings (see pages 148–51).

From Ravenna we headed south to San Marino, the world's oldest-surviving sovereign state (since the 4th century), situated on the slopes of Mount Titano. The local produce is spectacular there, particularly the amazing honey, which I combined with *panettone* in my Italian twist on bread and butter pudding (see page 218).

Riviera del Conero

My next stop was the Riviera del Conero, in Le Marche (a region sometimes known simply as Marche). The landscape is an enticing mix of sea, beaches, cliffs and gorgeous countryside, with the headland of Monte Conero dominating the area. The climate is conducive to supporting vineyards that produce *Rosso Conero*, a highly regarded local red wine. The pretty little town of Castelfidardo, which is nestled in the hills, is known as the birthplace of the accordion – and I got to play the world's largest working example.

When it comes to food, the quality and variety of ingredients in Marche is second to none and the cooking is traditional, with recipes passed on through the generations (see pages 120–21). With the province of Pesaro as the biggest truffle producer in Italy, the region also offers luxury foods for discerning gourmets worldwide.

The Tremiti Islands

Heading south, the next stage of my journey involved taking a short helicopter ride from Foggia to reach the Tremiti Islands, which form part of the Gargano National Park in northern Puglia. Looking down, you're immediately struck by the beauty and clarity of the emerald sea, which also happens to be one of Italy's most important areas of marine conservation. Only two of the five islands are inhabited: San Nicola, where the majority of the population is based, and San Domino, where you will find the only sandy beach in these islands. The smallest island (Pianosa) is often hidden by the tide. Besides a bit of snorkelling, I also got to spend time picking some fresh wild herbs, which, together with the fantastic local capers and fish caught that morning, came together in a really special dish (see page 49). Tourism is on the rise here, so now's the time to make a visit.

Polignano a Mare, Alberobello and Cisternino

Returning to the mainland, I travelled on to the beautiful region of Puglia (see pages 154–55). My first port of call was the stunning Polignano a Mare, another gem on the Adriatic coast, which is located just about where the 'heel' of Italy begins. It has everything you could want from an Italian seaside town – and that includes fabulous ice cream. In recent times, Polignano a Mare has become known for hosting the World Series of Cliff Diving; locals and tourists had been leaping into the crystal waters for years, but it's now become an event that attracts tens of thousands of spectators.

Heading inland, the town of Alberobello – white and gleaming under the hot Puglian sun – is famous for its distinctive *trulli* houses and is, understandably, a huge tourist destination. Characterised by their conical roofs, *trulli* can be found all over the region, but those of Alberobello are the best preserved, numbering in excess of 1,500 buildings. As a cook, I always associate Puglia with orecchiette (literally, 'little ears') – one of my favourite pasta shapes – so when I was in Alberobello I prepared *orecchiette con cime di rapa*, the most traditional of dishes in these parts (see page 101).

Also at the heart of Puglia's *trulli* region is Cisternino, officially designated one of Italy's most beautiful towns, with its charming architecture, shady streets and elegant squares. But most interesting to me were its *bombette Pugliesi*. These little 'bomb-shaped' pieces of meat (usually pork stuffed with local cheese and grilled or baked) are a speciality of the Itrian Valley, but many claim they originated in Cisternino.

Ostuni and Lecce

From Cisternino we headed southeast towards the spectactular town of Ostuni, about 8km from the coast. With its whitewashed, flat-topped buildings perched on top of a hill, the *città bianca* ('white town'), as it's sometimes referred to, is a dazzling sight. Ostuni is only 70km from Greece, and its architecture and labyrinth of tiny alleyways are very reminiscent of its southern neighbour.

In the search for great ingredients and a little R & R I booked in to the nearby *agriturismo* Masseria Montenapoleone – and it was just what I needed. An *agriturismo* is basically a farmhouse, but it's so much more than just a place to stay – it's the best way to experience Italian countryside and enjoy fresh, home-grown produce, in this case figs, apricots and almonds. I made the classic *spaghetti aglio, olio e peperoncino* for my host using the fantastic olive oil produced on the farm (see page 116).

Beautiful as the countryside was, we couldn't go to Puglia without visiting the elegant city of Lecce. Known as the 'Florence of the South', and renowned for its Baroque architecture, this is one of the most stunning cities in Italy. And for those with a sweet tooth, it's heaven on earth – ice cream parlours (*gelaterie*) and pastry shops (*pasticcerie*) are filled with goodies, including the famous local delicacy, *pasticciotto* (see page 213).

Journey's end

My last destination was Santa Maria di Leuca, at the tip of the heel of Italy, where the Ionian Sea meets the Adriatic. Its famous lighthouse dominates the bay, with the basilica, Santa Maria De Finibus Terrae ('end of the land'), alongside. I ended my journey out at sea, gazing back at this wonderful coastline and reflecting on what incredible places and people I had met on my journey – and of course all the amazing food I had enjoyed.

So this book is the culmination of my culinary journey. I want to share with you the dishes I discovered on my trip and bring a taste of Italy into your homes. The recipes are simple to prepare, look great and taste absolutely delicious. I am quite sure that you, your family and your friends will love them every bit as much as I do.

Buon appetito and *ciao*!

Gino xxx

Conversion tables

These are approximate conversions, which have been rounded up or down. Never mix metric and imperial measures in one recipe.

Weights
25g / 1oz
50g / 2oz
100g / 3½oz
150g / 5oz
200g / 7oz
250g / 9oz
300g / 10oz
400g / 14oz
500g / 1lb 2oz
1kg / 2¼lb

Volume (liquids)
5ml / 1 tsp
15ml / 1 tbsp
30ml / 1 fl oz / ⅛ cup
60ml / 2 fl oz / ¼ cup
75ml / ⅓ cup
120ml / 4 fl oz / ½ cup
150ml / 5 fl oz / ⅔ cup
175ml / ¾ cup
250ml / 8 fl oz / 1 cup
1 litre / 1 quart / 4 cups

Volume (dry ingredients)
Flour – 125g / 1 cup
Sugar – 200g / 1 cup
Butter – 225g / 1 cup
Breadcrumbs (fresh) – 50g / 1 cup
Grated cheese – 100g / 1 cup
Nuts (e.g. almonds) – 125g / 1 cup
Dried fruit (raisins, mixed peel, etc.) – 150g / 1 cup
Grains and small dried legumes (e.g. rice, lentils) – 200g / 1 cup

Lengths
1cm / ½ inch
2.5cm / 1 inch
20cm / 8 inches
25cm / 10 inches
30cm / 12 inches
35cm / 14 inches

Oven temperatures
140°C / 275°F
150°C / 300°F
160°C / 325°F
180°C / 350°F
190°C / 375°F
200°C / 400°F
220°C / 425°F
230°C / 450°F

Antipasti

The great tradition of sharing antipasti is long established in Italy, where meals can be very leisurely affairs – and the tasty starters in this chapter will suit any meal, anywhere.

Three cicchetti

Tre cicchetti

Cicchetti are part of the Venetian way of life – similar to Spanish tapas, they are tasty little snacks served in the local *bacari* (cicchetti bars). Bruschette with a wide variety of toppings are very popular, but other cicchetti include marinated seafood, salads and small meat dishes. They're best enjoyed with friends and a glass or two of chilled wine. I made these cicchetti for my fantastic gondolier, Riccardo, when we were filming the TV series. He seemed to enjoy them, and I hope you do too!

Serves 4
12 thin slices of ciabatta
4 tablespoons extra virgin olive oil
1 large garlic clove, peeled

For the nduja and ham bruschette
2–3 tablespoons nduja
4 large slices of Parma ham
Runny honey for drizzling
1 tablespoon shelled pistachio nuts, chopped

For the tomato and basil bruschette
160g fresh mixed cherry tomatoes, halved or quartered
Small handful of fresh basil leaves (about 30g), roughly torn
2 tablespoons extra virgin olive oil
Salt and freshly ground black pepper

For the prawn bruschette
8–12 raw king prawns, peeled and deveined
3 tablespoons mayonnaise
Pinch of chilli powder
1 tablespoon freshly squeezed lemon juice

1. First make the toasts. Preheat a ridged cast-iron chargrill pan over a high heat for 5–10 minutes. Meanwhile, drizzle or brush the oil over both sides of the ciabatta. When the pan is very hot, lay the ciabatta in the pan and grill for about 1 minute each side or until dark golden brown. Rub the garlic over 8 of the toasts, leaving 4 plain.

2. To make the nduja and ham bruschette, spread the nduja over the 4 plain toasts then lay the ham on top. Drizzle over a little honey and sprinkle over the pistachios.

3. To make the tomato and basil bruschette, put the tomatoes in a bowl with the basil and oil. Season with salt and pepper. Divide the mixture among 4 toasts.

4. To make the prawn bruschette, wipe the chargrill pan clean and return it to the heat. When very hot, lay the prawns in the pan and cook for about 2 minutes each side or until they turn pink and are lightly browned in places. Meanwhile, combine the mayonnaise and chilli powder in a small bowl. Add the lemon juice. Spread the mayonnaise over the remaining toasts then top each with 2 or 3 prawns.

Chargrilled plums with burrata, candied walnuts and mint pesto

Prugne grigliate con burrata, noci caramellate e pesto di menta

Burrata is an Italian cheese from Puglia, and it's become increasingly popular in Britain in recent years. It has a rich, milky, mozzarella-like shell and an oozing cream centre. I've used it here in a salad with a difference – the soft cheese combines perfectly with the griddled plums and peppery rocket, and the sweetened, earthy walnuts provide depth of flavour and a great texture. If you can't find burrata, use buffalo mozzarella instead.

Serves 4–6
25g unsalted butter
3 tablespoons caster sugar
100g walnut halves
8 plums, halved and stone removed
2 tablespoons extra virgin olive oil
90g rocket leaves
2 x 200g balls of burrata, drained

For the pesto
30g fresh mint
30g Parmesan cheese
30g toasted pine nuts
1 garlic clove, peeled
Juice of 1 lemon
100ml extra virgin olive oil
Salt and freshly ground black pepper

1. First make the pesto. Place the mint, Parmesan, pine nuts, garlic and lemon juice in a food processor. Season with salt and pepper. Blitz until finely chopped. Gradually add the oil in a steady stream and blend until smooth. Set aside.

2. Line a baking sheet with baking parchment. Heat a medium non-stick frying pan over a medium heat. When hot, add the butter, sugar and walnuts and fry for 7 minutes, stirring frequently, until the butter and sugar start to caramelise and coat the walnuts. Remove from the heat and tip immediately onto the prepared baking sheet. Set aside to cool.

3. Preheat a ridged cast-iron chargrill pan over a high heat for 5–10 minutes. Meanwhile, brush the plums with the oil and season with salt and pepper. Lay the plum halves cut-side down in the hot pan for 1 minute or until charred lines appear. Remove from the heat and set aside.

4. Spread out the rocket on a large serving platter. Roughly tear the burrata and scatter it over the rocket. Place the chargrilled plums on top. Sprinkle over the cooled walnuts, drizzle over the pesto and season with salt and pepper. Serve immediately.

Parma ham with courgettes, green beans and baby tomatoes

Prosciutto crudo con zucchine, fagiolini verdi e pomodorini

I tried this dish when filming in the region of Emilia-Romagna, where the famous Parma ham is produced. By law, prosciutto di Parma must be cured for a minimum of 12 months under specific traditional guidelines. The result is a distinctive and full flavoured ham that is both sweet and salty. This is a simple salad, but the fragrant dressing really brings out the flavours of the ham and vegetables. Leave the warm vegetables to cool in the dressing for at least 30 minutes so they can absorb the beautiful flavours.

Serves 4

350g baby courgettes, sliced lengthways into quarters
200g fine green beans, trimmed
200g fresh mixed baby tomatoes, quartered
12 slices of Parma ham

For the dressing

Juice of 1 lemon
2 garlic cloves, peeled and finely sliced
2 tablespoons chopped fresh mint, plus extra leaves to garnish
120ml extra virgin olive oil
Salt and freshly ground black pepper

1. Bring a medium saucepan of salted water to the boil. Add the courgettes and beans and bring back to the boil. Reduce the heat slightly and simmer for 3 minutes. Drain and set aside.

2. To make the dressing, put the lemon juice, garlic and mint in a large bowl. Gradually whisk in the olive oil, adding it in a steady stream. Season with salt and pepper.

3. Tip the warm courgettes and beans into the dressing and stir to coat. Add the tomatoes and toss everything together. Season with salt and pepper.

4. Lay 3 slices of Parma ham on each plate and pile the vegetables over and alongside the ham. Drizzle a little dressing over the ham and garnish with the mint leaves (sliced if they are large).

Barley salad with figs, roasted onions, olives and pecorino

Insalata di orzo perlato con fichi, cipolle al forno, olive e pecorino

When filming in Puglia I was served a small barley salad as part of an antipasti menu. Hearty and flavoursome, it's a real favourite in the region. This salad is now my 'go to' accompaniment when I barbecue fish. The flavours and textures complement each other so beautifully. Serve with a glass of chilled Italian white wine.

Serves 4–6

3 red onions, peeled and each cut into 8 wedges
2 teaspoons fennel seeds
2 tablespoons extra virgin olive oil
175g pearl barley, rinsed and drained
200g small ripe figs, quartered
150g pecorino cheese, roughly cut into bite-sized pieces
75g pitted green olives, drained

80g rocket leaves
Balsamic glaze to drizzle
Salt and freshly ground black pepper

For the dressing
2 tablespoons balsamic vinegar
Juice of ¼ orange
1 garlic clove, peeled and crushed
4 tablespoons extra virgin olive oil

1. Preheat the oven to 200°C/gas mark 6. Put the onions, fennel seeds and the oil in a large roasting tin, approximately 20 x 30cm. Season with salt and pepper and toss to coat. Roast for 35 minutes or until the onions are softened.

2. Meanwhile, put the barley in a medium saucepan and cover with cold salted water. Bring to the boil then reduce the heat. Partially cover the pan and simmer for 25 minutes. Drain and set aside.

3. To make the dressing, put the vinegar, orange juice and garlic in a small bowl and gradually whisk in the olive oil, adding it in a steady stream. Season with salt and pepper.

4. Remove the roasting tin from the oven. Add the figs, pecorino, olives and cooked barley and pour over the dressing. Toss together well.

5. Place the rocket on a large serving platter and arrange the contents of the roasting tin on the leaves. Drizzle over a little balsamic glaze.

Antipasti

Sea bream carpaccio with fennel, lemon and capers

Carpaccio di orata con finocchio, limone e capperi

When visiting Leuca, in Puglia, I found myself presented with a beautiful bream that was so fresh it would have been almost rude to cook it! So instead I made this deliciously delicate carpaccio. It's vital to use extremely fresh fish when serving it raw; bear in mind that spring tends to be the best time for sea bream. Serve with toasted ciabatta.

Serves 4

2 large or 4 small sea bream fillets (about 300g in total), pin-boned
2 fennel bulbs, cored and thinly sliced (reserve the fronds)
1 lemon
15g capers, drained
1 tablespoon extra virgin olive oil
Salt and freshly ground black pepper

1. Cover the sea bream in cling film and put in the freezer for about 20 minutes until firm but not frozen hard. Chill 4 flat serving plates.

2. Discard the cling film. Place the fish skin-side down on a board. Using a very sharp, long-bladed knife, slice at an angle across the grain into very thin slices, about the same thickness as smoked salmon. Discard the skin.

3. Arrange the sea bream slices on the chilled plates, spreading them out without overlap. Scatter the fennel slices over the fish.

4. Squeeze the juice from the lemon evenly over the fish, trying to get a few drops on every piece. Scatter over the capers and reserved fennel fronds and season with salt and pepper. Drizzle over the oil. Serve immediately.

Chicory filled with tuna and cannellini beans

Cicoria ripiena di tonno e fagioli cannellini

A versatile leaf, chicory can be eaten raw, baked, stir-fried or chargrilled. It can be either pale yellow-green or red, depending on the variety. There is little difference between the colours for flavour and texture – both are crisp with a bitter edge. I've chosen red chicory for this dish, as I wanted the more vibrant colour. The bitterness pairs well with tuna.

Serves 4–6

Juice of 1 lemon
2 tablespoons white wine vinegar
1 teaspoon Dijon mustard
100ml extra virgin olive oil
1 x 400g tin of cannellini beans, rinsed and drained
¼ red pepper, deseeded and finely chopped
½ celery stick, finely chopped
½ fennel bulb, cored and finely chopped
2 radishes, finely chopped
2 tablespoons chopped fresh flat-leaf parsley, plus extra to garnish
240g tuna chunks in oil (tinned or in a jar), drained
2 red chicory bulbs, leaves separated
Chilli oil for drizzling (see page 116)
Salt and freshly ground black pepper

1. Put the lemon juice, vinegar and mustard in a large bowl and gradually whisk in the olive oil. Season well with salt and pepper and add the beans. Using a spoon, mash the beans against the side of the bowl to break them up slightly.

2. Add the red pepper, celery, fennel, radishes and parsley to the bowl and stir. Mix in the tuna, trying not to break up the chunks too much. Season with salt and pepper.

3. Arrange 20 of the largest chicory leaves on a serving platter and fill each leaf with the tuna and bean filling.

4. Garnish with parsley and drizzle with a little chilli oil. Serve immediately.

Chicken livers on grilled polenta

Fegatini di pollo con polenta grigliata

All good Venetian restaurants have their own version of a liver and polenta dish on the menu – often calves' liver is used, but chicken livers are good too. Many pair theirs with creamed polenta, but I prefer to grill my polenta to give a crisp base that contrasts with the soft chicken livers. This dish makes a great antipasto, but it can also be served as a main course.

Serves 6 as a starter, 4 as a main course
250g chicken livers, trimmed
50g unsalted butter
50g Parma ham, finely chopped
1 tablespoon chopped fresh sage
50ml Marsala wine
1 tablespoon chopped fresh flat-leaf parsley
Salt and freshly ground black pepper

For the polenta
1 tablespoon extra virgin olive oil, plus extra for greasing
300ml full-fat milk
300ml hot vegetable stock
100g quick-cook polenta, plus 1 tablespoon for sprinkling
25g unsalted butter, cut into small cubes
1 tablespoon chopped fresh sage

1. First make the polenta. Lightly grease a shallow roasting tin, measuring about 20 x 30cm, with a little olive oil and set aside.

2. Heat the milk and stock in a medium saucepan over a high heat and bring to the boil. Reduce the heat to medium and gradually add the polenta, whisking continually until it starts to thicken and bubble. Simmer for 3 or 4 minutes, stirring, until it thickens further. Remove from the heat and stir in the butter and sage.

3. Spoon the cooked polenta into the prepared tin and smooth the surface. Set aside to cool then transfer to the fridge for 2 hours to set.

4. Preheat the grill to medium. Line a baking sheet with baking parchment. Turn out the polenta onto a board and cut in half lengthways. Slice each half into 5 rectangles, then cut each rectangle diagonally across to make 2 triangles.

You should have 20 triangles in total. Place the polenta triangles on the lined baking sheet and brush with the oil. Sprinkle over the extra polenta and place under the grill for 5–10 minutes or until lightly golden and crisp.

5. Meanwhile, season the chicken livers with salt and pepper. Melt the butter in a medium frying pan over a medium to high heat. Add the Parma ham and sage and fry for 1 minute, stirring continually. Add the chicken livers and fry for 4 minutes, turning halfway through cooking. Pour in the Marsala, bring to the boil and let it bubble for 30 seconds. Remove from the hob. Leave the chicken livers in the pan for 2–3 minutes to allow them to carry on cooking in the residual heat.

6. Arrange the polenta on a large serving plate. Spoon over the chicken livers and pan juices and scatter over the parsley. Serve immediately.

Food from Veneto

Located in northeastern Italy, Veneto extends from the Dolomite mountains in the north to Emilia-Romagna in the south, and from the Po Valley plains in the west to the Adriatic Sea in the east. Such geographical diversity has resulted in a rich, highly varied cuisine.

The region's capital, Venice, has had a major impact on the cooking of the area. For centuries a powerful city-state and marine republic, with trade links around the world and a wealthy cosmopolitan population, Venice has long had refined tastes and strong culinary traditions that spread far and wide. Exotic foods imported from the East and northern Europe by explorers and merchants were distributed inland, where they were integrated into the local cooking, and soon many imports – including rice, maize and wheat – began to be cultivated in the region. Despite the dominance of Venetian cuisine, individual localities in Veneto have managed to retain their own distinct culinary traditions.

Fish & seafood

Along the Adriatic coast, including in the lagoon city of Venice, the local diet is based largely on fish and seafood. Clams, mussels, prawns and cuttlefish are all proudly displayed in markets and restaurants. A speciality of the Veneto area is *stoccafisso* (stockfish), or dried cod that has been air-dried without salt. Confusingly, this is sometimes referred to as *baccalà*, which elsewhere in Italy refers to salted dried cod. One traditional dish that I had to feature in this book is *sarde in saor* (marinated sweet and sour sardines, see page 30). You really should try it.

Meat, poultry & game

As in most of Italy, pork is widely enjoyed in Veneto – fresh and cured, in sausages and salamis. However, beef is also popular, either in stews, grilled or sliced thinly as carpaccio. In the plains, meat is often grilled on a barbecue. Locals also like poultry and wild fowl, such as guinea fowl or duck. There are many species of wild duck in the Po Delta, sometimes served with bigoli pasta (see opposite).

Polenta

The most common dish throughout Veneto is polenta. Once classed as the poor man's staple, polenta is now featured on every restaurant menu in the region and is cooked in various ways. It is usually made from maize, which was introduced from the Americas in the 15th to 16th centuries and has been cultivated in the region since the 17th to 18th centuries.

Traditionally, polenta was prepared (and often still is) by constantly stirring cornmeal, water and salt over heat for 40 minutes with a wooden stick called a *mescola*. Fortunately, you can now buy quick-cook polenta, which saves you time and your arm muscles! In Veneto, you will find polenta served as a side dish for meat in its creamy form, or as a solid block – sliced and toasted, fried or grilled. Polenta is often served with *stoccafisso*, braised beef, *ragù* – or even as a dessert. One of the most popular dishes is *fegato alla Veneziana* (calves' liver with sage served with polenta). I have included my own version on page 25.

Rice & pasta

One of the earliest imports to Italy was rice, which came from Asia and was introduced to Europe via Spain. It has been grown in Italy since the 15th century, with the Po Valley being the main rice-growing area in the country.

In Veneto, rice is more popular than pasta. It is always cooked with other ingredients. The classic Venetian rice dish is *risi e bisi*, which is made with rice and young, fresh peas and has the consistency of a thick soup. Risotto is also very popular in Veneto, particularly made with fish and seafood, but sometimes with vegetables, offal, wild fowl and frogs' legs. It is always made with Italian long-grain rice, and absorbs the liquid in which it is cooked. It has a creamy but not mushy consistency.

There are few traditional pasta dishes from Veneto, but the most popular shape is bigoli, which resembles thick, coarse-textured spaghetti. It used to be made with buckwheat flour, and sometimes contains duck eggs, but today is usually made using wholewheat flour. Traditionally, it was made by hand using a brass press known as a *bigolaro*.

Vegetables

Radicchio, or red chicory, with its crisp red leaves and slightly bitter taste, is prized in the Veneto region and is used in rice dishes, grilled as a vegetable, cooked in soups or eaten raw in salads. *Radicchio rosso di Treviso* (which is mainly used in cooking) and *radicchio rosso di Chioggia* (which is mainly used in salads) are regional favourites. Asparagus is another popular vegetable in Veneto, especially *asparagi di Bassano* – a white asparagus that is usually boiled and served with vinaigrette or eggs. Small artichokes are often eaten raw and dipped in olive oil.

Sweets & cakes

One of the most famous Venetian cakes is the *pandoro* – a traditional sweet yeast bread, not dissimilar to a *panettone*, which is most commonly eaten around Christmas and New Year. One of tastiest local sweet treats is *fritole Veneziane* (see page 216) – small fried doughnuts that are sold everywhere in the lead-up to the *Carnevale di Venezia*. Of course, I can't get away with not also mentioning the famous *tiramisù*. This classic coffee-flavoured dessert is said to have originated in Veneto, and is now known around the world. I love to make this dessert, but with a few variations on the traditional version (see page 203).

Sautéed prawns with garlic and chilli

Gamberoni saltati in padella con aglio e peperoncino

Many restaurants along the Adriatic coast of Italy offer their own version of this deliciously spicy prawn dish. It looks and tastes so decadent, yet is so incredibly easy to prepare. I like to use the biggest prawns I can get my hands on, but smaller ones will work just as well – just adjust the quantities and cooking time accordingly. Serve with crusty bread.

Serves 4

2 large garlic cloves, peeled and thinly sliced

2 fresh, medium-hot red chillies, deseeded and finely chopped

100ml olive oil

16–20 raw king prawns (ideally about 50–60g each), peeled and deveined

Juice and zest of 1 unwaxed lemon

3 tablespoons chopped fresh flat-leaf parsley

Salt

1. Put the garlic and chillies in a large frying pan. Add the oil and place the pan over a medium heat. As soon as the garlic starts to sizzle, add the prawns and fry for 3 minutes on each side. Season with salt.

2. Add the lemon juice and zest and 2 tablespoons of the parsley and toss everything together. Fry for 1 minute, stirring continuously.

3. Transfer the prawns to a large serving platter and drizzle the sauce over the top. Sprinkle over the remaining tablespoon of parsley. Serve immediately.

Sweet and sour sardines

Sarde in saor

This is a typical Venetian dish, which can be found in almost every restaurant in Venice. Before modern refrigeration was invented, saor (the technique of marinating in vinegar) was a favourite method of food conservation. This recipe has been passed down through the generations and really stands the test of time. Traditionally it contains pine nuts, but I prefer flaked almonds. Serve hot, or prepare ahead, chill overnight and bring to room temperature before serving. Here I've chargrilled the sardines, but you can also cook them under the grill if you prefer. Serve with toasted ciabatta or grilled polenta.

Serves 4
½ unwaxed lemon
8 fresh whole sardines, descaled, gutted
  and washed
8 sprigs of fresh rosemary
2 tablespoons olive oil
½ onion, peeled and thinly sliced

80ml dry white wine
80ml white wine vinegar
30g raisins
1 sprig of fresh thyme
10g flaked almonds
Salt and freshly ground black pepper

1. Cut the half lemon into 8 thin slices, then cut each slice in half. Stuff 2 halves into each fish cavity and add a sprig of rosemary. Pat the sardines dry with kitchen paper and brush each side with oil (about 1 tablespoon in total). Season with salt and pepper.

2. Preheat a ridged cast-iron chargrill pan over a high heat for 5–10 minutes. When very hot, lay the sardines in the pan and cook for 3 minutes each side, without moving the fish around in the pan. Set aside on a serving platter.

3. Heat the remaining 1 tablespoon of oil in a small saucepan over a low to medium heat. Add the onion and fry for 8 minutes or until softened, stirring occasionally. Increase the heat to high. Pour in the wine and vinegar, bring to the boil and let it bubble for about 2 minutes until slightly reduced.

4. Add the raisins and thyme and season with salt and pepper. Simmer for 2 minutes. Pour the sauce over the sardines and sprinkle over the almonds.

Baked artichokes with an oozing cheese and herb filling

Carciofi al forno con ripieno di formaggio fuso ed erbe

Artichokes are popular all over Italy. We just adore them! There are many different varieties and the way we cook them varies from region to region; they can be marinated or served with a simple dressing for antipasti, stuffed with cheese or meat (see page 67) or added to pasta. I especially love this dish; the blended cheeses become hot and creamy and form a delicious individual dip inside each artichoke.

Serves 4

4 large globe artichokes
3 unwaxed lemons, halved
150g Gorgonzola cheese
50g mascarpone cheese
50g ricotta cheese, drained
1 garlic clove, peeled and crushed

1 tablespoon chopped fresh oregano
2 tablespoons chopped fresh flat-leaf parsley
15g fresh white breadcrumbs
1 tablespoon extra virgin olive oil
Salt and freshly ground black pepper

1. Bring a large saucepan of salted water to the boil. Meanwhile, clean the artichokes and remove the dark, tough outer leaves. Using a sharp knife, cut off the top third of each artichoke and trim the stalk close to the artichoke's base. Using scissors, trim the sharp points from any remaining outer leaves.

2. Plunge the artichokes into the boiling water. Squeeze the juice from the lemons into the pan and add the spent shells. Bring back to the boil then reduce the heat to medium. Cover and cook for about 30 minutes or until tender (they are ready when you can easily pull out a leaf from the centre with a slight tug).

3. Line a plate with kitchen paper. Using a slotted spoon, lift out the artichokes and place them upside down on the plate to drain.

4. Meanwhile, in a medium bowl combine the cheeses, garlic, oregano and half the parsley. Season with salt and pepper.

5. In a small bowl combine the breadcrumbs and remaining parsley. Preheat the oven to 180°C/gas mark 4.

6. Once the artichokes are cool enough to handle, gently prise open the leaves to expose the hairy choke at the centre. Using a teaspoon, scoop out the choke and discard.

7. Arrange the artichokes snugly in a small baking dish and fill the centres with the cheese mixture. Sprinkle over the breadcrumbs and drizzle over the oil. Bake for 25 minutes or until the cheese has melted and the crumbs are golden brown. Serve immediately.

Beef and barley soup

Zuppa di orzo perlato e manzo

Barley has been cultivated in Italy since ancient times. It was believed to give fighters extra strength – gladiators were known as the *hordearii*, or 'barley eaters', and Roman soldiers used to march off to war with a bag of barley, which they boiled up in their helmets to make porridge. Barley is great in soups, adding a nice bite, and here it absorbs the rich flavour of the beef stock. Serve with plenty of fresh crusty bread.

Serves 4

50g pearl barley, rinsed and drained
800ml hot beef stock
1 tablespoon extra virgin olive oil
1 onion, peeled and finely chopped
2 celery sticks, finely sliced
2 carrots, peeled and finely chopped
1 turnip, peeled and finely chopped

1 fresh, medium-hot red chilli, deseeded and finely sliced
2 tablespoons chopped fresh oregano, plus whole leaves to garnish
250g lean sirloin steak, cut into thin strips
1 x 400g tin of chopped tomatoes
Salt

1. Put the pearl barley and stock in a medium saucepan over a medium heat and bring to the boil. Reduce the heat, cover and simmer for 10 minutes.

2. Meanwhile, heat the oil in a large saucepan over a medium to high heat. Add the onion, celery, carrots, turnip, chilli and oregano and fry for 5 minutes, stirring occasionally. Add the beef and fry for 2 minutes, stirring continually.

3. Pour the stock and barley into the pan with the vegetables and beef. Add the tomatoes and bring to the boil. Reduce the heat, cover and simmer for 30 minutes. Remove the lid and skim off and discard any fat and residue that has risen to the surface. Re-cover and cook for a further 30 minutes. Season with salt.

4. Ladle into warm bowls and garnish with the oregano leaves.

Fish & seafood

It's no surprise that fish and seafood figure prominently on menus and household tables along the Adriatic coast. Here is a selection of favourites from the region, all of which you can easily cook at home.

Smoked mackerel and beetroot salad with mascarpone and dill dressing

Insalata di sgombro affumicato e barbabietola rossa
al mascarpone ed aneto

Dill isn't a traditional Italian herb, but I felt the need for something aromatic and delicate in this creamy dressing. It complements the earthy flavour of the beetroot beautifully. Smoked mackerel fillets are readily available in supermarkets and are relatively inexpensive. They're also nutritiously rich in Omega-3 and vitamins. Try to buy smaller beetroot, as the larger ones can take a long time to cook.

Serves 4 as a starter, 2 as a main course
400g beetroot (about 4–6), trimmed
2 green chicory bulbs, leaves separated
230g smoked mackerel fillets, skinned

For the dressing
60g mascarpone cheese
4 tablespoons double cream
2 tablespoons semi-skimmed milk
1 teaspoon Dijon mustard
Juice and zest of 1 unwaxed lemon
2 tablespoons chopped fresh dill, plus extra sprigs to garnish
Salt and freshly ground black pepper

1. Preheat the oven to 200°C/gas mark 6. Place the beetroots in the centre of a large square of foil and add 2 tablespoons of water. Bring the sides of the foil up and scrunch the ends together to form a loose but tightly sealed parcel.

2. Place the parcel on a baking sheet and transfer to the oven for 45–60 minutes or until the beetroot is tender when pierced with the end of a knife. Leave to cool.

3. Meanwhile, make the dressing. Put all the ingredients in a small bowl and stir to combine. Season with salt and pepper and set aside.

4. Arrange the chicory leaves on a large serving platter. Break the mackerel into bite-sized pieces and scatter it over the chicory.

5. Once the beetroots are cool enough to handle, slip them out of their skins and cut into wedges. Arrange on the plate with the chicory leaves and mackerel.

6. To serve, drizzle over the dressing, grind over some black pepper and garnish with dill sprigs.

Lobster salad with baby tomatoes and celery in a hard-boiled egg dressing

Insalata di aragosta, pomodorini e sedano con salsa alle uova sode

Italians love lobster, and we were treated to some of the freshest I've ever tasted when filming along the Adriatic coast. This recipe shows off the delicate flavour of the lobster, allowing it to be the star of the dish. If you would rather not handle live lobsters, you can buy them already cooked from many larger supermarkets. Serve with crusty bread.

Serves 4
2 live lobsters (each about 600g)
2 medium eggs
Juice of 1 lemon
Juice of 1 orange
½ teaspoon dried chilli flakes
150ml extra virgin olive oil

250g fresh mixed baby tomatoes, halved
3 celery sticks, sliced diagonally into
  1cm lengths
3 tablespoons chopped fresh flat-leaf
  parsley
Salt and freshly ground black pepper

1. Make some air holes in a large plastic bag, place the lobsters in the bag and seal. Transfer immediately to the freezer for 45 minutes. Bring a large saucepan of salted water to the boil. Drop in the lobsters head first and cook for 8–10 minutes. Lift out with tongs and set aside to cool.

2. Meanwhile, place a small saucepan of water on the hob and bring to the boil. Lower the eggs into the pan and bring the water back to the boil. Reduce the heat to medium and simmer gently for 10 minutes. Lift out the eggs and plunge them into a bowl of cold water. Peel when cool enough to handle. Leave to cool.

3. Remove the meat from the lobsters. First twist off the large claws. Using a nutcracker, the back of a heavy knife or a rolling pin, crack the claw shells. Pick out the meat and put it in a bowl.

4. Place one lobster body shell on a board, belly-side down. Using a heavy, sharp knife, split the lobster in half lengthways, cutting from the head to the tail. Pull the halves apart. Discard the intestinal tract from the tail and the stomach sac. Remove the meat from the shell and cut into 2cm chunks. Put in the bowl with the claw meat. Discard the shell. Repeat with the second lobster.

5. Chop the cooled eggs and place in a large bowl. Add the lemon juice, orange juice and chilli flakes. Season with salt. Add the olive oil gradually, whisking all the time, until the yolks become smooth.

6. Add the tomatoes, celery and parsley and stir to coat. Add the lobster meat and toss together until evenly coated. Grind over a little black pepper and serve.

Prawn, kale and asparagus salad with anchovy dressing

Insalata di gamberoni, cavolo riccio e asparagi con salsa alle acciughe

Kale has recently become popular in Britain as a health food due to its high volume of antioxidants and nutrients, but in Italy it has long been a staple ingredient. The typical Italian kale is Tuscan kale or cavolo nero (black cabbage), but for this recipe I have used green curly kale. This is a great salad to prepare ahead because the flavours intensify over time.

Serves 4
1 garlic clove, peeled and crushed
1 tablespoon olive oil
350g raw king prawns, peeled and deveined
200g fine asparagus spears, woody ends removed and halved across
160g chargrilled artichokes hearts in olive oil, roughly chopped (reserve the oil)
150g curly kale, tough central midribs removed and roughly chopped
25g roasted, chopped hazelnuts
Salt and freshly ground black pepper

For the dressing
4 anchovy fillets in oil, drained
50ml full-fat milk
Juice from 1 lemon
1 garlic clove, peeled and crushed
1 teaspoon Dijon mustard
1 teaspoon runny honey
4 tablespoons extra virgin olive oil

1. Put the garlic in a medium frying pan. Add the oil and place over a medium to high heat. As soon as the garlic starts to sizzle, add the prawns, season with salt and fry for about 5 minutes, stirring occasionally, until they have turned pink and are cooked through. Using a slotted spoon, transfer the prawns to a large serving bowl.

2. Bring a medium saucepan of salted water to the boil. Drop in the asparagus and cook for 3 minutes or until cooked but with some bite. Drain and plunge immediately into cold water to refresh. Drain again and leave to cool.

3. Meanwhile, make the dressing. Put the anchovies in a ramekin, pour over the milk and leave to soak for 10 minutes (this makes them less salty). Drain and discard the milk. Finely chop the anchovies.

4. Put the anchovies in a medium bowl. Add the lemon juice, garlic, mustard and honey. Gradually whisk in the olive oil and 2 tablespoons of oil from the artichokes. Season with pepper.

5. Put the asparagus, artichokes and kale in the bowl with the prawns. Drizzle over the dressing and stir well. Sprinkle over the hazelnuts and stir again. Season with salt and pepper.

Swordfish steaks and sautéed potatoes with gremolata

Tranci di pesce spada con patate saltate e gremolata

I cooked this dish overlooking the beach at Pescoluse, on the Puglian coast. It's known as the Maldives of Salento and is a hidden paradise. I used swordfish, but tuna would work well too. Gremolata is a dressing of raw chopped garlic, parsley and lemon zest. It is usually sprinkled over meats, such as osso bucco or carpaccio, but it also makes a great garnish for grilled fish. Always make sure you buy swordfish from a sustainable source, from fisheries that have been certified by the Marine Stewardship Council (MSC).

Serves 4
1kg new potatoes, scrubbed
180ml olive oil
8 sprigs of fresh rosemary
6 garlic cloves, bruised with the back of a knife
4 x 175g swordfish steaks

For the gremolata
12 tablespoons chopped fresh flat-leaf parsley
2 large garlic cloves, peeled and finely chopped
1½ tablespoons capers, drained and roughly chopped
Juice and zest of 1 unwaxed lemon
100ml extra virgin olive oil
Salt

1. Bring a large pan of salted water to the boil and cook the potatoes for about 7 minutes then drain. When the potatoes are cool enough to handle, slice in half lengthways.

2. Meanwhile, make the gremolata. Put the parsley, garlic, capers and lemon juice and zest in a medium bowl. Pour in the oil and stir to combine. The mixture should have the texture of a wet pesto. Season with salt. Set aside.

3. Heat 90ml of the oil in a large, high-sided frying pan or sauté pan over a medium to high heat. When very hot, add half the potatoes, cut-side down. Fry for about 1 minute then add the rosemary and 4 of the garlic cloves. Fry the potatoes for about 5 minutes each side or until golden and crisp. Transfer to kitchen paper to drain. Repeat with the remaining potatoes, topping up with more oil if needed. Keep warm.

4. Meanwhile, heat the remaining 90ml of the oil in a large, non-stick frying pan over a high heat. When hot, add the remaining 2 garlic cloves. Gently lay the swordfish steaks in the pan and fry for 2 minutes each side, or until the fish is just cooked through. Season with salt.

5. Divide the potatoes among 4 serving plates and place the swordfish alongside. Drizzle over the gremolata.

Squid with borlotti beans, chilli and spinach

Calamari con borlotti, peperoncino e spinaci

Every year the seaside town of Pinarella di Cervia in Ravenna holds a week-long festival dedicated to the wonders of the squid. Visitors come from all over Italy, and once they're in Emilia-Romagna they discover the other fabulous ingredients and dishes the region has to offer (see pages 82–83).

Serves 4

6 fresh whole squid
2 tablespoons olive oil
1 x 400g tin of borlotti beans, rinsed and drained
1 x 400g tin of chopped tomatoes
4 fresh sage leaves
1 garlic clove, peeled and finely sliced
1½ fresh, medium-hot red chillies, deseeded and finely chopped
40ml dry white wine
150g fresh spinach, thick stalks removed
Juice of 1 lemon
3 tablespoons extra virgin olive oil
1 tablespoon chopped fresh flat-leaf parsley
Salt and freshly ground black pepper

1. To prepare the squid, pull the tentacles from the body. Feel inside the body and remove and discard the 'quill' (a transparent sliver of cartilage). Wash the inside of the body and peel off the outer skin. Cut off the squid tentacles just below the eyes (discard the head and guts). Discard the small, hard 'beak' at the base of the tentacles. Rinse the tentacles in cold water.

2. Cut each body pouch in half lengthways and open out. Score the inner side with the tip of a sharp knife into a fine diamond pattern. Brush both sides of the pouch and the tentacles with the olive oil. Set aside.

3. Put the beans, tomatoes, sage, garlic, one third of the chillies and the wine in a medium saucepan over a medium heat. Bring to the boil then reduce the heat and simmer for 10 minutes.

Remove the sage and discard, then tip in the spinach and cook for 3 minutes or until wilted, stirring occasionally. Add half the lemon juice and the extra virgin olive oil. Season to taste. Stir to mix and keep warm.

4. Season the squid pouches and tentacles with salt and pepper. Heat a large frying pan over a medium heat. Add the squid (the pouches scored-side down) and fry for 1 minute until golden brown. Turn over and add the parsley and remaining lemon juice and chilli. You may need to fry in batches. Remove the squid from the pan and cut into bite-sized pieces. Return it to the pan and toss to coat.

5. Spoon the bean and spinach mixture into a serving bowl. Arrange the squid on top and pour over any pan juices. Serve immediately.

Prawn and monkfish soup

Brodetto

Once considered poor man's food, Italian fish soup can now be found in the best restaurants along the Adriatic coast. From Trieste to Puglia you'll find the so-called brodetti (broths), although they vary from region to region. We had countless bowlfuls on our coastal journey; each was unique and all were delicious. Here I've used prawns and monkfish, but any white fish would work just as well. Serve with plenty of fresh crusty bread for dunking.

Serves 4
2 tablespoons olive oil
1 onion, peeled and finely chopped
75g diced smoked pancetta
1 celery stick, finely chopped
1 fennel bulb, cored and finely chopped
1 carrot, peeled and finely chopped
1 x 400g tin of chopped tomatoes
100ml dry white wine
400ml hot fish stock

5 fresh basil leaves, shredded, plus whole
   leaves to garnish
1 tablespoon chopped fresh flat-leaf
   parsley, plus extra for garnish
500g skinless monkfish fillets, roughly
   chopped into bite-sized pieces
100g large raw prawns, peeled and
   deveined
Salt and freshly ground black pepper

1. Heat the oil in a medium pan over a medium heat. Add the onion and fry for 5 minutes, stirring occasionally. Add the pancetta, celery, fennel and carrot and fry for 2 minutes, stirring.

2. Increase the heat to high. Add the tomatoes, wine, stock, basil and parsley and bring to the boil. Reduce the heat to medium. Simmer for 10 minutes, stirring occasionally, and season with salt and pepper.

3. Reduce the heat to low and add the monkfish. Simmer very gently for 5 minutes, stirring occasionally, then add the prawns and cook for 5 minutes. Ladle the soup into bowls and garnish with parsley and basil leaves.

Fish & seafood

Meat & poultry

Although seafood is king on menus along the coast, meat is also very popular. Here I've included slow-cooked stews, roasts and grills as well as super-quick, last-minute recipes. There's something for every occasion.

Sliced steak with chargrilled pears and tomatoes, walnuts, Gorgonzola and Parmesan

Tagliata con pere e pomodori grigliati, noci, Gorgonzola e Parmigiano

Tagliata is steak that has been carved into slices and is usually served on a bed of leaves. It's a great way to serve meat when you're entertaining, as it's perfect for sharing, looks impressive yet is really simple and quick to cook. I love rib-eye steak – the rich marbling of the meat guarantees it's tasty and succulent – but sirloin can be used as an alternative. Remember to remove the meat from the fridge 30 minutes before cooking.

Serves 4

3 rib-eye steaks (about 225g each), room temperature
3 tablespoons olive oil
40g fresh rosemary
2 pears (ideally slightly under-ripe), cut into large chunks
16 fresh red cherry tomatoes on the vine

90g rocket leaves
1 head of radicchio, leaves torn into large chunks
60g walnut pieces, roughly chopped
200g Gorgonzola cheese, crumbled
Parmesan cheese shavings to serve
Balsamic glaze to serve
Salt and freshly ground black pepper

1. Preheat a large ridged cast-iron chargrill pan or heavy-based frying pan over a high heat for 5–10 minutes.

2. Pat the steaks dry with kitchen paper and rub oil over both sides. When the pan is very hot, carefully lay the steaks in the pan. Cook for about 2 minutes, pressing down with a fish slice but not moving the steaks around. Turn over and cook for 1 minute on the other side for rare (2 for medium rare). You will probably have to cook the steaks in two batches.

3. Meanwhile, arrange half the rosemary on a plate or in the bottom of a dish. When the steaks are cooked, lay them on top of the rosemary. Cover with the remaining rosemary and leave to rest for 5 minutes.

4. Reduce the heat and put the pears in the chargrill pan. Add the tomatoes. Cook for a few minutes or until lightly marked and just starting to soften.

5. Season the steaks with salt and pepper. Slice into strips 1cm wide, slightly on the diagonal.

6. Scatter the rocket over a serving platter, then the radicchio. Arrange the steak, tomatoes, and pear on top. Finish with the walnuts, Gorgonzola and Parmesan shavings (use a vegetable peeler to shave the cheese). Drizzle over some balsamic glaze and the cooking juices.

Baked artichokes stuffed with spicy mince in a tomato sauce

Carciofi al forno ripieni di macinato piccante con salsa al pomodoro

Italy is the world's largest producer of artichokes and it's easy to see why; the soil is rich and the sun is plentiful – the best way to an artichoke's heart! Used frequently in dishes from Marche, Abruzzo and Puglia, artichokes are so versatile and have a sweet, nutty flavour. This recipe uses just the artichoke bases – you can find them in large supermarkets or delis and they really are a great addition to your store cupboard. Serve with rice and a mixed salad.

Serves 4

2 large garlic cloves, peeled and halved
3 tablespoons olive oil
2 x 400g tins of chopped tomatoes
5 fresh basil leaves, roughly torn
2 teaspoons salt
8–10 artichoke bottoms from a jar, drained
Extra virgin olive oil for drizzling

For the filling

500g lean beef mince
1 garlic clove, peeled and crushed
1 tablespoon tomato purée
1 teaspoon dried chilli flakes
1 tablespoon chopped fresh flat-leaf parsley, plus extra to garnish
1 tablespoon shredded fresh basil
Salt

1. Preheat the oven to 160°C/gas mark 3. Put the garlic in a medium saucepan. Add the olive oil and place the pan over a medium heat. As soon as the garlic starts to sizzle, add the tomatoes, basil and salt and bring to the boil.

2. Reduce the heat and simmer for 8 minutes or until reduced and thickened. Pour into a baking dish, about 20 x 30cm.

3. Put the ingredients for the filling in a medium bowl. Mix thoroughly to combine and season with salt.

4. Place the artichoke bottoms on top of the tomato sauce and fill the centre of each with the filling mixture. Bake for 35 minutes.

5. Drizzle with a little extra virgin olive oil and garnish with parsley. Serve immediately.

Meat & poultry

[67]

Roasted rib of beef with garlic and herbs

Costata di manzo al forno con aglio ed erbe

Some of the best Italian beef is farmed in the southeastern region of Marche. The cattle are allowed to roam free, and the meat from *Marchigiana* cattle is appreciated all over the country. Rib of beef is perfect for a special occasion; it's so delicious that it really doesn't need a lot doing to it. Serve with Creamy potato and fennel bake (see page 179) and enjoy with a glass of Italian red wine.

Serves 4–6

3kg rib of beef (2 bones)
4 tablespoons extra virgin olive oil
6 large garlic cloves, peeled and crushed
1 tablespoon chopped fresh oregano
1 tablespoon chopped fresh flat-leaf parsley
1 tablespoon chopped fresh thyme
1 tablespoon wholegrain or English mustard
1 tablespoon salt
Freshly ground black pepper

1. Preheat the oven to 230°C/gas mark 8. Lay the beef in a large roasting tin, bone-side down.

2. In a small bowl put the oil, garlic, herbs, mustard and salt. Season with pepper and stir to combine. Rub the mixture into the beef to coat.

3. Roast for 30 minutes then reduce the oven temperature to 190°C/gas mark 5. Cover the beef with foil and roast for a further 50 minutes.

4. Remove the tin from the oven and wrap the beef snugly in an extra sheet of foil. Leave to rest for 20 minutes.

5. Remove the foil and carve the beef into slices. Serve immediately.

Beef fillet with green peppercorns, sage and lemon

Filetto di manzo al pepe verde, salvia e limone

When visiting Burano, an island in the Venetian lagoon, for the TV series we saw this dish on many restaurant menus. They tended to include both sage and rosemary in the recipe, but I prefer to use just the sage as the combination can be quite overpowering. Because fillet is expensive, I've suggested a small piece of meat for this recipe, but feel free to increase the quantities. Serve with a rocket and Parmesan salad.

Serves 2–3

500g beef fillet (room temperature)
1 tablespoon olive oil
160ml extra virgin olive oil
2 tablespoons green peppercorns in brine, drained

16 fresh sage leaves
1 unwaxed lemon
Salt

1. Preheat the oven to 160°C/gas mark 3. Brush the beef all over with the olive oil.

2. Heat a medium frying pan over a high heat. When the oil is very hot, sear the meat for 1–2 minutes each side – it should be brown all over but still rare in the middle.

3. Meanwhile, put the extra virgin olive oil, green peppercorns and sage in a small saucepan. Place over a low heat. Peel 4 large pieces of zest from the lemon and add to the oil. Keep warm so the flavours can infuse.

4. Transfer the beef to a baking sheet and roast for 8 minutes (for rare beef).

5. Remove the beef from the oven and cover with foil. Leave to rest for 5 minutes. Season with salt.

6. Slice the beef into thin slices and arrange on a serving platter. Remove the lemon zest from the oil and discard. Pour the infused oil over the beef. Serve immediately.

Roast lamb with baby new potatoes, carrots and Jerusalem artichokes

Agnello arrosto con patatine novelle, carote e topinambur

Garlic and rosemary are the flavours most associated with roasting lamb in Italy, and the taste is hard to beat, but the addition of a few anchovies lifts the flavour to a whole new level. Here I've paired my lamb with some roasted vegetables. You can substitute these vegetables for your favourites, but please try to include some Jerusalem artichokes. Their subtle, smoky flavour permeates the other vegetables beautifully.

Serves 4

1 shoulder of lamb (about 1.5kg), deboned
4 tablespoons olive oil
10 garlic cloves, peeled and bruised with the back of a knife
6 anchovy fillets in oil, drained
4 sprigs of fresh rosemary

150ml dry white wine
2 carrots, peeled, halved widthways and quartered lengthways
300g baby new potatoes
300g Jerusalem artichokes, peeled and halved lengthways
Salt and freshly ground black pepper

1. Preheat the oven to 240°C/gas mark 9. Season the lamb with salt and pepper. Heat 2 tablespoons of the oil in a large, flameproof casserole or high-sided frying pan over a high heat. When very hot, sear the lamb for about 2 minutes each side or until brown. Using a slotted spoon, transfer the lamb to a roasting tin, about 30 x 20cm.

2. Add 6 of the garlic cloves, the anchovies, 2 sprigs of rosemary and the wine to the tin. Cover the tin tightly with foil. Reduce the oven temperature to 160°C/gas mark 3 and roast for 2 hours.

3. Meanwhile, bring a medium saucepan of salted water to the boil. Add the carrots, potatoes and Jerusalem artichokes and bring back to the boil. Reduce the heat and simmer for 10 minutes. Drain thoroughly.

4. About 30 minutes before the lamb is ready, put the remaining 2 tablespoons of oil into a slightly smaller roasting tin, about 25 x 20cm. Add the remaining 4 garlic cloves and 2 sprigs of rosemary. Tip the drained vegetables into the dish, season with salt and pepper and stir to coat. Put the roasting tin in the oven and roast for 40 minutes, stirring halfway through cooking.

5. About 10 minutes before the lamb is done, remove the foil and roast uncovered.

6. Remove the lamb from the oven and leave to rest for 15 minutes. Slice the lamb and serve alongside the vegetables.

Puglian lamb stew

Stufato di agnello alla pugliese

You'd have probably expected me to cook a seafood dish when visiting the picturesque cove of Polignano a Mare, in Puglia. However, despite facing the sea, the absence of safe moorings for boats has prevented the development of a fishing tradition in the town, so it relies on agriculture. The area is famous for its wonderful fresh vegetables – especially salad, olives and potatoes – so I decided to combine local produce with lamb to make this delicious stew. This dish is definitely one of the highlights from my latest TV series – it's comforting, delicious and easy to make. Serve with toasted ciabatta.

Serves 4

4 tablespoons olive oil
2 large red onions, peeled and thinly sliced
1kg boned leg of lamb, trimmed and cut into 3cm cubes
4 celery sticks, chopped into 3cm lengths and leaves finely sliced
3 sprigs of fresh thyme
2 bay leaves
3 small unwaxed oranges (zest of 1 and juice of 3)

90g pitted black olives, drained
3 tablespoons runny honey
400ml full-bodied red wine
1 x 400g tin of chopped tomatoes
200ml hot vegetable stock
3 medium potatoes, peeled and cut into large chunks
150g frozen peas, defrosted
Salt and freshly ground black pepper

1. Heat the oil in a large flameproof casserole over a medium heat. Add the onions and fry for 5 minutes or until softened and browned, stirring occasionally.

2. Increase the heat. Add the lamb, season with salt and pepper and fry for about 5 minutes. Reduce the heat. Add the celery, thyme, bay leaves, orange zest, olives and honey and fry for 5 minutes or until caramelised.

3. Increase the heat. Pour in the wine and allow it to bubble for about 2 minutes or until reduced by one third.

4. Add the tomatoes and orange juice. Bring to the boil then reduce the heat and simmer for 1 hour, partially covered with a lid.

5. Add the stock and the potatoes and bring back to the boil. Partially cover again and simmer for a further 45 minutes or until the meat and potatoes are tender.

6. Stir in the peas and celery leaves and leave to rest for a few minutes off the heat before serving.

Barbecued leg of lamb with chilli, honey, rosemary and garlic

Cosciotto di agnello al barbeque con peperoncino, miele, rosmarino e aglio

Barbecued lamb just doesn't get better than this. When Italians barbecue, we don't use overpowering sauces or rubs, but instead stick to traditional herbs and other ingredients that enhance the flavours of the meat. If you prefer, the meat can be cooked in the oven at 200°C/gas mark 6 for 40–45 minutes. Serve with a tomato and red onion salad.

Serves 6–8
1 leg of lamb (2kg), deboned and butterflied
5 garlic cloves, peeled and thinly sliced
20g fresh rosemary leaves
2 tablespoons extra virgin olive oil

2 fresh, medium-hot red chillies, deseeded and finely chopped
2 tablespoons runny honey
1 tablespoon balsamic vinegar
Juice of 1 lemon
Salt

1. Light the barbecue. Meanwhile, make shallow incisions in the lamb on the skin side with a small, sharp knife, leaving a 3cm gap between each incision. Push a garlic slice and a few rosemary leaves into each cut. The lamb will take about half the rosemary. Brush the lamb with the oil and season with salt.

2. When the barbecue is ready (the coals will be covered in a fine greyish white ash), put the lamb on the barbecue. Cook for 15 minutes, turning it over every 5 minutes until nicely charred (and turning it over if it starts to catch).

3. Meanwhile, make the basting sauce. Strip the remaining leaves from the rosemary, reserving the stalks, and finely chop the leaves. Put them in a small bowl and add the chillies, honey, vinegar and lemon juice. Stir to combine.

4. Move the lamb to a raised rack on the barbecue and throw the reserved rosemary stalks onto the direct heat underneath the lamb.

5. Brush the lamb with half the sauce and put the lid on the barbecue. Cook for 10 minutes, turning if necessary. Brush over the remaining sauce and cook for a further 5–10 minutes or until the lamb is cooked as you like it.

6. Remove the lamb from the barbecue, cover with foil and leave to rest for 10 minutes before carving into slices.

Food from Emilia-Romagna

The region of Emilia-Romagna, with its capital of Bologna, is often considered to be one of the gastronomic highlights of Italy. It consists of two different areas – Emilia in the west and Romagna to the east, on the Adriatic. The cuisine of the two parts differs, but there are many shared characteristics.

The land in Emilia-Romagna is very rich and fertile and offers perfect grazing land for cattle. As a result, butter and lard are often used in cooking instead of olive oil. The coastline is also one of the top fish-producing areas in Italy. The region is famous for a number of staple Italian ingredients, most notably Parmesan cheese, Parma ham and balsamic vinegar.

Fish & seafood

On the coast, seafood forms a large part of the locals' diet. Mussels are harvested not far offshore in the Adriatic Sea and are used in many local pasta dishes. Eels from the Comacchio lagoon are considered a delicacy all over Italy, and clams and sole are frequently seen on restaurant menus. As in other regions along the Adriatic coast, *brodetto* (fish soup) is popular. I have included my version on page 61.

Meat & poultry

Emilia-Romagna is a big meat-eating region. Pork is the most popular meat, but chicken and lamb are also widely enjoyed.

The craft of curing meats is held in high esteem in Emilia-Romagna and the regional *salumi* are famous throughout the world. Some of the more popular products include *mortadella*, *pancetta* and *culatello di Zibello*, a local delicacy. Parma ham is probably Italy's most famous pork product. The careful balance of quality ingredients and a long, completely natural ageing process result in a distinctive sweetness and an exquisite, delicate flavour.

Pasta

The food of choice in this region is pasta, particularly fresh egg and stuffed pasta. The favourites include tortellini, tagliatelle, cannelloni, lasagne, farfalle, cappelletti, tortelli and anolini. Of course, Emilia-Romagna is also the birthplace of Bolognese sauce, known in Italy simply as *ragù*. Stuffed pasta, such as tortellini, is often served as a first course before a meat main course, particularly on special occasions such as Christmas Eve. Pasta here is not just a savoury affair – sweet pastas may be served as a dessert or as a side dish.

Cheese

Emilia-Romagna has a strong cheese-making tradition – the abundance of pastures in the fertile Po Valley means milk and butter are of exceptional quality. It's no wonder that this is the birthplace of the highly prized Parmesan cheese. The provinces of Parma, Reggio and Emilia have had legal title to the production of *Parmigiano Reggiano* for hundreds of years and by law it can be produced only in this region. Another famous cheese of this part of Italy, and one that is highly regarded in the gastronomic world, is *formaggio di fossa*, which is left to age for three months in a pit. Fossa can be eaten by itself, grated on pasta or – better still – with honey.

Balsamic vinegar

Emilia-Romagna has produced balsamic vinegar since Roman times, and it is used in Italy to flavour all kinds of cooking, from salads and meat to fruit salads and ice cream. There are three protected types, which are strictly regulated and must be produced in the region. The best-quality vinegars are *aceto balsamico tradizionale di Modena* and *aceto balsamico tradizionale di Reggio Emilia*. They are made from grape must and are aged for at least 12 years, often for considerably longer. The result is a delicious, aromatic, syrupy vinegar.

There is also a less expensive, commercial-grade product, *aceto balsamico di Modena*, which is made from grape must mixed with wine vinegar and is aged for a minimum of two months. Caramel is added to mimic the sweetness of the traditional aged vinegars.

Chestnuts

Chestnuts are popular throughout Italy, but the forests in the mountains of Emilia-Romagna (especially the area of Frignano) are particularly known for their abundance of this delicious nut. Years ago, chestnuts were a necessary food for poor families living in the mountains. Today, roasted or sweetened chestnuts are enjoyed as a treat in autumn and winter. They are also widely used in soups, risottos (see page 134), breads and desserts, as well as in flour for baking.

Fennel

Both cultivated and wild fennel feature prominently in Italian cooking and are particularly popular in Emilia-Romagna. The bulbs and the fronds are used, both raw and cooked, in side dishes, pastas, salads, gratins and risottos. Fennel seed is also a common ingredient in Italian sausages and other meat products. I love fennel – it goes perfectly with pork, fish or chicken, so I've included two recipes in which fennel is the star of the dish (see pages 172 and 179).

Piadina

A speciality of Emilia-Romagna, *piadina* is a flat wheat bread that can be served hot or cold and either topped with ingredients (see page 149) or filled with meats and cheeses, like a wrap or sandwich (see page 151). As a sweet treat it can also be filled with Nutella! *Piadina* kiosks can be found all over the region and the bread has become a staple of Romagna's street-food scene.

Barbecued skewered pork meatballs

Spiedini di polpette di maiale al barbeque

I love cooking outside on a barbecue. A beer in hand with friends and family by my side is cooking as it should be. These pork meatballs are perfect for a barbecue party – they're easy to make, inexpensive and delicious. If you don't have a barbecue, or if it isn't barbecue season, cook the meat under a hot grill for about 12 minutes, turning halfway through cooking.

Serves 4

6 tablespoons extra virgin olive oil
30g fresh white breadcrumbs
500g lean pork mince
1 fresh, medium-hot red chilli, deseeded and finely chopped
4 tablespoons chopped fresh flat-leaf parsley
2 tablespoons chopped fresh thyme
1 garlic clove, peeled and crushed
1 egg, lightly beaten
1 red pepper, deseeded and cut in half across and 8 lengthways (i.e. 16 chunks)
1 large onion, cut in half across and 8 lengthways (i.e. 16 chunks)
1 large courgette, cut in half lengthways and 8 across (i.e. 16 half moons)
2 tablespoons balsamic vinegar
Salt and freshly ground black pepper

1. Soak 8 wooden skewers, about 25cm long, in cold water for at least 30 minutes. Alternatively, use metal skewers. Line a baking sheet with foil.

2. Heat 2 tablespoons of the oil in a small frying pan over a medium to high heat. Add the breadcrumbs and fry, stirring constantly, for 3 minutes or until the breadcrumbs start to turn golden and crisp. Transfer to a bowl. Set aside.

3. In a large bowl, combine the pork, chilli, parsley, thyme, garlic, beaten egg and toasted breadcrumbs. Season with salt and pepper. Mix with your hands until thoroughly combined.

4. Using dampened hands, take small amounts of the pork mixture and roll into 24 balls, each weighing about 25g each. Place the balls on the lined baking sheet. Cover and transfer to the fridge for at least 30 minutes.

5. Light the barbecue. Thread the skewers as follows: red pepper, meatball, onion, courgette, meatball, onion, courgette, meatball, red pepper.

6. Put the vinegar in a small bowl and lightly whisk in the remaining 4 tablespoons of oil. Season with salt and pepper. Using a pastry brush, coat the skewered meatballs and vegetables with the mixture.

7. When the barbecue is ready (the coals will be covered in a fine greyish white ash), place the skewers on the barbecue and grill for 5–6 minutes. Using tongs, carefully turn over the skewers and cook for a further 5–6 minutes or until the pork is cooked all the way through.

8. Pile the skewers onto a large serving platter, season with salt and pepper and serve immediately.

Pork chops with tomatoes, fennel, red pepper, raisins and capers

Braciole di maiale con pomodoro, finocchio, peperone rosso,
uvetta e capperi

This is my idea of a rustic, healthy, 'throw it in the pan' recipe and is inspired by my journey through Marche. Pork and fennel is a popular combination in this region, and I think it works perfectly in this dish together with the piquancy of the capers and sweetness of the raisins and honey. It's ideal for a tasty mid-week supper because it doesn't take much time or effort.

Serves 4
4 boneless pork chops (about 800g total)
4 tablespoons olive oil
2 fennel bulbs, cored and cut into 8
  wedges
1 onion, peeled and thinly sliced
1 red pepper, deseeded and roughly
  chopped
1 celery stick, thinly sliced
3 tablespoons chopped fresh flat-leaf
  parsley

100ml dry white wine
1 tablespoon runny honey
1 x 400g tin of chopped tomatoes
1 tablespoon tomato purée
50g raisins
Zest of 1 unwaxed lemon
3 tablespoon capers, drained
Salt and freshly ground black pepper

1. Season the pork with salt and pepper. Heat the oil in a large saucepan or shallow flameproof casserole over a medium to high heat. When very hot, add the pork and fry for about 4 minutes each side or until brown all over. Remove with a slotted spoon, transfer to a large bowl or plate and cover with foil. Set aside.

2. Reduce the heat to medium. Add the fennel, onion, red pepper, celery and 2 tablespoons of the parsley to the pan. Fry for 5 minutes, stirring occasionally.

3. Increase the heat and add the wine and honey. Cook for 1 minute, scraping any caramelised bits off the bottom of the pan.

4. Stir in the tomatoes, tomato purée and raisins. Bring to the boil then reduce the heat. Return the pork to the pan and push it down so it is mostly submerged in the juices. Simmer for 15 minutes or until the pork is cooked through.

5. Remove the pork and place on 4 warm serving plates. Stir the lemon zest, capers and remaining 1 tablespoon of parsley into the vegetables and season with salt and pepper. Spoon the vegetables alongside the pork and serve immediately.

Fillet of pork with root vegetables and capers

Filetto di maiale con ortaggi a radice e capperi

Pork is Italy's favourite white meat, particularly when prepared as cured meat and salami. Italians use the whole pig, from snout to tail, but in this recipe I'm using only the beautiful fillet. I've combined it with parsnips, carrots and onions, but celery, swede, potato or any other root vegetables would work just as well. This recipe is a foolproof dish to serve as a Sunday roast. Serve with creamy polenta.

Serves 4–6

2 x 500g pork fillets
3 tablespoons olive oil
200ml dry white wine
2 onions, peeled and quartered
2 parsnips, peeled and cut into chunks
2 carrots, peeled and cut into chunks

650ml hot vegetable stock
1 tablespoon runny honey
2 bay leaves
30g capers, drained
Salt and freshly ground black pepper

1. Preheat the oven to 200°C/gas mark 6. Season the pork with salt and pepper. Heat the oil in a large flameproof casserole over a high heat. When very hot, sear the meat for 2 minutes each side or until browned. Using a slotted spoon, transfer the meat to a large plate or bowl and set aside.

2. Pour the wine into the casserole and bring to the boil. Let it bubble for 1 minute, scraping all the caramelised bits from the bottom of the pan.

3. Add the onions, parsnips, carrots, stock, honey and bay leaves. Cover, transfer the casserole to the oven and cook for 30 minutes. Add the pork and cook for a further 20–25 minutes or until the meat and vegetables are tender.

4. Using a slotted spoon, transfer the vegetables to a large serving dish and cover with foil. Remove the pork and place it on a board, cover with foil and leave to rest for 5 minutes.

5. Return the casserole to the hob over a high heat, bring to the boil and simmer for 5 minutes to reduce the sauce.

6. Carve the pork into thick slices and lay the meat on the vegetables. Pour over a little of the sauce and sprinkle over the capers. Put the remaining sauce in a jug and serve on the side.

Roast chicken in a herb-salt rub

Pollo arrosto al sale aromatizzato con erbe

This dish requires a little bit of planning because the salt rub needs to be prepared at least 24–48 hours in advance of cooking, but it's well worth it. Although you might think the chicken would taste too salty, it doesn't; instead the result is a super-juicy bird with a crispy skin. Cooking salt is used to cure meats and fish and is slightly stronger than ordinary sea salt. Serve with my Potato and herb fritters (see page 182) and a side salad.

Serves 4
500g cooking salt
4 garlic cloves, peeled and finely sliced
2 tablespoons chopped fresh sage
1 tablespoon chopped fresh rosemary

2 tablespoons chopped fresh oregano
1 whole chicken (about 1.75kg)
2 onions, peeled and sliced horizontally
 into 4 pieces
Freshly ground black pepper

1. To make the rub, put the salt in a bowl and add the garlic, herbs and a good grinding of black pepper. Mix well and cover loosely with a piece of kitchen paper. Set aside for 2 days, stirring a couple of times a day.

2. Massage the rub into the chicken skin; avoid getting the salt in the cavity. Cover and chill for about 4 hours.

3. Remove the chicken from the fridge 30 minutes before cooking. Meanwhile, preheat the oven to 220°C/gas mark 7.

4. Arrange the onions in a single layer in the centre of a large roasting tin to make a base for the chicken. Using a pastry brush, remove as much salt from the chicken as you can. Place the chicken breast-side down on the onions.

5. Transfer to the oven and roast for 15 minutes, then turn and cook for a further 15 minutes. Reduce the temperature to 180°C/gas mark 4 and cook for a further 50 minutes.

6. Remove from the oven, cover with foil and leave to rest for 10 minutes before carving.

PECORINO
PICCANTE

Pasta, rice & gnocchi

This chapter is bursting with deliciousness. It includes a range of pasta dishes, comforting risottos and a silky-smooth gnocchi dish that simply caresses your taste buds …

Linguine with asparagus and toasted pine nuts

Linguine con asparagi e pinoli tostati

I look forward to the asparagus season in Italy – partly because I love eating it, but also because it heralds the spring, with the promise of long, warm days ahead. I've made a silky smooth sauce using a similar method to a carbonara for this dish, and the addition of fresh asparagus and toasted pistachios works brilliantly. Give it a try and let me know what you think!

Serves 4

50g shelled pistachio nuts
2 garlic cloves, peeled and crushed
1 tablespoon olive oil
500g dried linguine
500g fine asparagus spears, woody ends removed and sliced diagonally into 2cm lengths

6 medium egg yolks
180g freshly grated Parmesan cheese, plus extra to serve
2 tablespoons snipped fresh chives (optional)
Salt and freshly ground black pepper

1. Preheat the oven to 180°C/gas mark 4. Put the pistachios on a baking sheet and roast for 7 minutes, then leave to cool. Crush the pistachios coarsely with a rolling pin. Set aside.

2. Put the garlic in a small frying pan. Add the oil, place the pan over a medium heat and fry the garlic for 1 minute. Set aside.

3. Cook the linguine in a large pan of boiling, salted water. After about 5 minutes, drop in the asparagus. Reserve a cupful of the cooking water. Continue to cook the linguine with the asparagus until the pasta is al dente then drain.

4. Meanwhile, lightly whisk the egg yolks with half the Parmesan and 6 tablespoons of the reserved cooking water. Season with salt and black pepper.

5. Tip the pasta and asparagus back into the pan they were cooked in. Off the heat, add the egg yolk mixture, cooked garlic, remaining Parmesan and the chives, if using. Mix everything together for 30 seconds (the heat from the pasta will be sufficient to cook the egg to a creamy texture). Stir in the crushed pistachios.

6. Transfer to warm bowls, sprinkle over some extra Parmesan and grind over some black pepper.

Paccheri with four cheeses

Paccheri ai quattro formaggi

Originating from Campania and Calabria, paccheri is a popular pasta shape in the region of Marche. When filming there I made this dish using a selection of delicious cheeses. This is a tasty and filling meal that's really easy to make – it's my version of a posh macaroni cheese! If you can't find paccheri you can use large rigatoni for this recipe. If scamorza is unavailable, use a mixture of ordinary mozzarella and smoked Cheddar.

Serves 4

400g dried paccheri
100g Gorgonzola cheese, cut into small pieces
100g Taleggio cheese, rind removed and cut into small pieces
100g scamorza (smoked mozzarella) cheese, rind removed and cut into small pieces
3 tablespoons full-fat milk
1 tablespoon extra virgin olive oil
2 tablespoons chopped chives
2 teaspoons sweet paprika
80g freshly grated pecorino cheese
Freshly ground black pepper

1. Cook the paccheri in a large pan of boiling, salted water until al dente.

2. Meanwhile, put the Gorgonzola, Taleggio and scamorza in a large saucepan. Add the milk, oil, half the chives and the paprika. Place the pan over a medium to low heat to melt the cheeses and stir to combine. Do not allow the mixture to boil. Remove from the heat and season with a little pepper.

3. When the paccheri is cooked, remove it from the water using a slotted spoon and put it directly into the sauce without draining. Ensure some of the cooking liquid comes along with it. Gently fold the pasta through the sauce and stir in half the pecorino.

4. Transfer the pasta to individual serving plates or bowls. Sprinkle over the remaining pecorino and remaining chives and serve immediately.

Crab and prosecco linguine

Linguine al granchio e prosecco

Venice's Rialto Fish Market is a vibrant, bustling place full of amazing fresh produce. I loved the atmosphere – all the locals out shopping and the fishmongers loudly calling out their catch of the day. These guys start work so early that they can often be seen enjoying their lunch with a glass of prosecco by 9am! So you can see where I found the inspiration for this recipe. Fresh crab is paired with the subtle flavour of prosecco to create a delicious celebratory dish; one that I was lucky enough to enjoy with all the beauty of Venice as my backdrop. If you prefer, use dry white wine instead of prosecco.

Serves 4

500g dried linguine
4 tablespoons olive oil
4 garlic cloves, peeled and finely chopped
1 fresh, medium-hot red chilli, deseeded and finely chopped
200g fresh red cherry tomatoes, halved
Zest of 2 unwaxed lemons
150–200ml prosecco
360g fresh white crab meat
120g pitted green olives, drained and halved
6 tablespoons chopped fresh flat-leaf parsley
Salt

1. Cook the linguine in a large pan of boiling, salted water until al dente.

2. Meanwhile, put the oil, garlic and chilli in a large, high-sided frying pan or sauté pan and place over a medium heat. Fry gently for about 1 minute, stirring continuously.

3. Add the tomatoes and cook for 2 minutes or until slightly softened (you do not want them to turn mushy). Stir in the lemon zest. Season with salt.

4. Increase the heat and pour in the prosecco. Bring to the boil and let it bubble until almost evaporated (about 1–2 minutes). Add the crab meat, olives and parsley and turn off the heat.

5. When the linguine is cooked, remove it from the water using tongs or a spaghetti spoon and put it directly in the pan with the crab mixture without draining. Gently toss the pasta to ensure it is evenly coated. Serve immediately.

Spaghetti with garlic, olive oil and chillies

Spaghetti aglio, olio e peperoncino

Spaghetti aglio, olio e peperoncino is a classic Italian dish – simple to cook and full of flavour. I cooked it for Giuliano and his family to thank him for letting us stay at his wonderful *agriturismo* in Ostuni. It was the perfect choice to show off his fantastic olive oil. The chilli oil in this recipe is optional, but I really recommend making a batch as it keeps well (up to 12 months if stored in an airtight container in a cool, dark place) and has so many uses. For example, it's great for pepping up pizzas and breads as well as pasta dishes, or for frying prawns. Make it at least 12 hours ahead so the flavours have a chance to blend.

Serves 4
500g dried spaghetti
100ml extra virgin olive oil
5 garlic cloves, peeled and chopped
8 tablespoons chopped fresh flat-leaf parsley
2 teaspoons dried chilli flakes
1 fresh, medium-hot red chilli, finely sliced (seeds left in)

For the chilli oil
600ml olive oil
5 teaspoons dried chilli flakes
2 teaspoons chilli powder
20 small whole dried red chillies

1. To make the chilli oil, pour the olive oil into a clean, sterilised bottle or glass jar. Add the remaining ingredients, seal with a tight-fitting lid and shake well. Leave for at least 12 hours.

2. Cook the spaghetti in a large pan of boiling, salted water until al dente.

3. Meanwhile, pour the oil into a large, high-sided frying pan or sauté pan. Add the garlic, parsley, chilli flakes and chilli and place the pan over a medium to high heat.

4. As soon as the ingredients start to sizzle, stir and fry for about 1 minute, stirring continuously. Remove from the heat.

5. When the spaghetti is cooked, return the frying pan to a medium heat. Transfer the pasta to the frying pan without draining, using tongs or a spaghetti spoon. Stir for 30 seconds to allow the flavours to combine. Drizzle over a little chilli oil, if using. Serve immediately.

Spaghetti with red mullet, tomatoes, olives, capers and spicy pangrattato

Spaghetti con triglia rossa, pomodorini, olive, capperi e pangrattato piccante

I created this dish, which is perfect for a light lunch or dinner, when we were filming on the coast of Puglia. Red mullet is particularly popular in the region and is cooked in so many different ways – fried, baked, or added to soups, risottos or pasta. Pangrattato is a toasted breadcrumb topping, which adds texture and flavour to pasta and risotto dishes. I love how its crunchiness complements the delicate fish and silky pasta in this recipe.

Serves 4

400g dried spaghetti
2 garlic cloves, peeled and thinly sliced
6 tablespoons olive oil
100g pitted black olives, drained
60g capers, drained
300g fresh mixed baby tomatoes, quartered
8 small red mullet fillets (about 300g in total), skinned and pin-boned
2 tablespoons chopped fresh flat-leaf parsley

4 tablespoons extra virgin olive oil
Salt and freshly ground black pepper

For the pangrattato
100g stale ciabatta bread (at least 1 day old)
Large pinch of dried chilli flakes
Zest of 1 unwaxed lemon
2 tablespoons olive oil

1. First make the pangrattato. Put the ciabatta, chilli flakes and lemon zest in a food processor and blitz to fine to medium crumbs. Heat the oil in a medium frying pan over a medium heat. Add the crumbs and fry for about 3–4 minutes, stirring continuously, until golden and crisp. Season with salt and pepper. Set aside.

2. Cook the spaghetti in a large pan of boiling, salted water until al dente.

3. Meanwhile, put the garlic in a large, high-sided frying pan or sauté pan. Add the olive oil and place the pan over a medium to high heat. As soon as the garlic starts to sizzle, add the olives, capers and tomatoes and fry for 3 minutes, stirring continuously. Lay the red mullet on the vegetables in a single layer and add half the parsley. Cook gently for 2 minutes. Remove from the heat.

4. Once the spaghetti has finished cooking, remove with tongs and place on top of the fish. Place the pan over a low heat, drizzle over the extra virgin olive oil and gently toss everything together. Season with salt and pepper.

5. Transfer the pasta to 4 warm plates and sprinkle over the pangrattato and the remaining parsley. Serve immediately.

Pasta, rice & gnocchi

Food from Le Marche

Situated in central-eastern Italy, Le Marche (often known simply as Marche) is nestled between the Apennine Mountains in the west and the Adriatic Sea to the east. The region is often overlooked by visitors, yet it has so much to offer – hills and mountains, quaint villages, sweeping vistas, 180 kilometres of coastline with many beautiful sandy beaches, and great food.

The cuisine of Marche is based on the quality of the raw ingredients – meat, dairy, vegetables, fish and seafood of all kinds. The region has a rich culinary tradition, with specialities that have remained the same for centuries – some dating back to ancient Roman times. There is an emphasis on home cooking rather than a restaurant culture – although this is changing over time – with recipes handed down through families for generations.

One of the key characteristics of *Marchigiano* cuisine is a love of stuffed dishes, including elaborately stuffed vegetables – particularly cauliflower and courgettes – stuffed olives and stuffed pasta. However, possibly the most well-known pasta dish in Marche is *vincisgrassi*, which is a rich version of lasagne.

Fish & seafood

The Adriatic Sea off the Marche coast is rich with seafood, including many types of shrimps, cuttlefish and squid – all of which feature prominently in local dishes. The Portonovo wild mussels that live attached to the rocks of Conero were once fished by the locals and removed with pitchforks; now their fishing is closely regulated to preserve the stock. In and around Ancona and the Conero Riviera you will find *brodetti*, or fish soups (see page 61), on every restaurant menu. They are prepared with all types of fish and seafood and other ingredients like garlic, paprika and saffron. Traditionally, the soups were made by the port workers from leftovers and unwanted scraps that couldn't be sold at the market, but today they are very much a celebrated dish. Red mullet is particularly popular in the region (see pages 58 and 119).

Meat & game

Meat is readily available in Marche because of the quality of the pastureland, and the locals are very much meat-lovers. Dishes vary from pigeon and wild fowl to marinated lamb. Nothing is wasted and every part of the animal is used – from the head to the trotter. As always in Italy, pork is the meat of choice, and *porchetta* (roast suckling pig) is a favourite. Pork and fennel is a popular combination, either in sausages or cooked or served together (see Pork chops with tomatoes, fennel, red pepper, raisins and capers, page 86).

Cheese

Pecorino cheese, especially young pecorino, is the most favoured cheese of Marche, and some excellent varieties are produced here. Made from sheep's milk, pecorino is similar to Parmesan and is often used to dress pasta dishes when you want a sharper, slightly stronger flavour. Other cheeses of note include *casciotta d'Urbino*, a velvety sheep's milk and cow's milk cheese, which is hand-pressed into rounds that are then salted and cured in a moist environment, and the earthy-tasting *ambra di Talamello*, made from sheep's, goat's or cow's milk and cured in a pit lined with straw.

Vegetables & fruit

Marche has an ideal climate for growing vegetables and fruit, and is known for its artichokes, apricots, pears and peaches. Olives grow well here and are used both for olive oil and for eating. A popular local dish is *olive all'Ascolana* – green olives stuffed with meat, coated in breadcrumbs and fried.

Artichokes are very much celebrated in the region, so much so that there is an annual festival dedicated to the vegetable. The *Sagra del Carciofo*, or Artichoke Festival, which is held in Montelupone in May each year, is visited by thousands and showcases all things artichoke with food stalls and dinners. Italians adore artichokes and use the many different varieties in a number of

ways. I've included a few recipes in this book to show off this much-loved vegetable (see pages 35, 45, 67, 76 and 125).

Figs

Marche is one of the biggest fig-growing regions in Italy, and this popular fruit is eaten raw or baked. Dried figs are a special delicacy, prepared with candied peel and almonds and compressed to form bricks or cylinders. A tasty local speciality is *lonzino di fico* – it may look like salami, but it's actually made from sweet dried fruit: figs, almonds, walnuts and star anise, wrapped in fig leaves. I've created a dessert for this book, inspired by the popular combination of figs and almonds (see page 204).

Truffles

The province of Pesaro, in Marche, is the biggest truffle producer in Italy, particularly of the highly prized white truffle, which is one of the most expensive foods in the world. Each autumn, the famous *Sagra del Tartufo*, or Truffle Festival, is held in Acqualagna. Visitors come from all over the world to taste and buy.

Wine & liqueurs

One of the most well-known wines of Marche is *Verdicchio*, a white wine from the hills that pairs well with fish, and the local red wine *Rosso Conero*, which is made with the Montepulciano grape – perfect with pork and chocolate. The region is also famous for *anisetta*, an aromatic liqueur that smells and tastes like anise.

Tagliatelle with watercress and walnut pesto topped with olives

Tagliatelle al pesto di crescione e noci con guarnizione di olive

Vibrant and fresh, this sauce makes a delicious alternative to the more traditional basil pesto. It is also packed with nutrients and antioxidants from the watercress. I love the peppery kick of watercress and it perfectly complements the earthy taste of the walnuts and the creamy mascarpone. If you cover the pesto with a layer of olive oil and store it in the fridge it will last for up to one week.

Serves 4
500g dried tagliatelle
200g watercress, plus extra leaves to garnish
½ garlic clove, peeled
80g freshly grated Parmesan cheese, plus extra to serve (optional)

75g mascarpone cheese
70g walnut pieces
50g pitted black olives, halved
Extra virgin olive oil for drizzling
Salt and freshly ground black pepper

1. Cook the tagliatelle in a large pan of boiling, salted water until al dente.

2. Meanwhile, make the pesto. Put the watercress (including stalks and leaves), garlic, Parmesan, mascarpone and 50g of the walnuts in a food processor and blitz until smooth. Season with salt and pepper.

3. Drain the pasta and tip it back into the pan. Pour over the pesto and stir together for 30 seconds to combine.

4. Transfer to a warm serving bowl. Scatter over the olives and remaining walnuts. Drizzle with a little oil and sprinkle over some extra Parmesan, if using. Garnish with watercress leaves.

5. Add the artichoke hearts and stock. Season with salt and pepper. Bring to the boil then reduce the heat and cover. Simmer gently for about 10 minutes. Blend until smooth and stir in 30g of the Parmesan.

6. Spread half the artichoke purée over the base of a baking dish, about 20 x 30cm.

7. Stand the paccheri upright in the sauce. Using a teaspoon, fill the paccheri with the vegetable and passata mixture; push the mixture down into the bottom of the tube using the handle of the spoon. Cover the paccheri with the remaining artichoke purée.

8. Sprinkle over the remaining 20g Parmesan and the breadcrumbs. Bake for 25 minutes or until golden brown. Just before serving, sprinkle with the parsley.

Pasta bake with spicy chicken, tomatoes and spinach

Pasta al forno con pollo piccante, pomodori e spinaci

Taking inspiration from the region of Puglia, this dish features one of my favourite pasta shapes – orecchiette. We tried a similar baked pasta dish when filming in Alberobello and I just had to make my own version when I returned home. Orecchiette literally means 'small ears' and it's a perfect shape for soaking up delicious sauces like this one. If you can't find orecchiette, use penne rigate or fusilli instead. Serve with a green salad.

Serves 4–6

2 tablespoons olive oil

1 onion, peeled and roughly chopped

2 x 400g tins of chopped tomatoes

1 tablespoon chopped fresh oregano

1 teaspoon sugar

2 teaspoons salt

230g fresh spinach, thick stalks removed

350g dried orecchiette

4 skinless, boneless chicken breasts, cut into strips

1 teaspoon chilli powder

For the cheese sauce

100g salted butter

100g plain flour

1 litre full-fat milk

50g freshly grated Parmesan cheese

¼ teaspoon freshly grated nutmeg

Salt and freshly ground pepper

For the topping

25g fresh white breadcrumbs

2 tablespoons chopped fresh flat-leaf parsley

10g freshly grated Parmesan cheese

1. Heat 1 tablespoon of the oil in a medium saucepan over a medium heat. Add the onion and fry for 5 minutes or until slightly softened.

2. Add the tomatoes, oregano, sugar and 1 teaspoon of the salt and bring to the boil. Reduce the heat, cover and simmer for 15 minutes, then remove the lid and simmer for a further 15 minutes. Remove from the heat and blend until smooth.

3. Return to the heat then add the spinach. Cook until wilted for about 3 minutes, stirring occasionally. Set aside.

4. Cook the orecchiette in a large pan of boiling, salted water for 4 minutes less than stated on the packet. Drain, refresh in cold water and leave to drain again. Preheat the oven to 180°C/gas mark 4.

5. Put the chicken in a medium bowl with the chilli powder. Add the remaining 1 tablespoon of oil and 1 teaspoon of salt. Stir well to ensure all the chicken is evenly coated. Heat a large frying pan over a medium to high heat. Add the chicken and fry for about 4 minutes or until golden brown, turning halfway through cooking. Set aside.

6. Make the cheese sauce. Melt the butter in a large saucepan over a medium heat until foaming. Add the flour and cook for 1–2 minutes or until pale golden, stirring continuously. Gradually add the milk, a little at a time, whisking constantly and waiting for it to be incorporated before adding more.

7. Bring to the boil then reduce the heat and simmer gently for about 5–10 minutes, continuing to whisk, until thickened and smooth. Remove from the heat and stir in the Parmesan and nutmeg. Season with salt and pepper. Set aside to cool slightly.

8. Tip the cooled pasta back into the pan it was cooked in and stir in the tomato and spinach mixture.

9. Combine the ingredients for the topping in a small bowl. Season with salt and pepper.

10. Pour half the cheese sauce into a baking dish, about 20 x 30cm, then spoon over half the pasta, tomato and spinach mixture. Lay the chicken on top. Spoon over the rest of the pasta, tomato and spinach mixture then pour over the remaining sauce. Sprinkle over the topping. Bake for 25 minutes or until golden brown.

Pasta, rice & gnocchi

Saffron risotto with balsamic-glazed, chargrilled chicken

Risotto allo zafferano con pollo grigliato alla crema di balsamico

Santa Maria di Leuca sits on the southernmost tip of the Salento peninsula, where the waters of the Adriatic mix with those of the Ionian Sea. A popular resort for wealthy Puglians since the early 1900s, Leuca is both beautiful and rich in history. During filming I had the honour of cooking this dish for the priest, Don Gianni, and the nuns in the grounds of the Basilica of Santa Maria De Finibus Terrae.

Serves 4

2 skinless, boneless chicken breasts
5 tablespoons olive oil
3 tablespoons balsamic glaze
1 large red onion, peeled and chopped
300g Arborio or Carnaroli rice
½ tablespoon fresh thyme leaves, plus extra sprigs to garnish
About 12 saffron threads
150ml dry white wine
1 litre hot vegetable stock
80g salted butter, cut into cubes
80g freshly grated pecorino cheese
Salt and freshly ground black pepper

1. Lay a chicken breast between 2 sheets of cling film. Using a meat mallet or heavy-based saucepan, pound the chicken to about 1.5cm thick. Repeat for the other chicken breast. Drizzle 1 tablespoon of oil over the 2 breasts.

2. Preheat a large ridged cast-iron chargrill pan over a high heat for 5–10 minutes. Once hot, lay the chicken in the pan and season with salt and pepper. Cook for about 3 minutes each side or until golden.

3. Drizzle over a little balsamic glaze then turn and cook for about 30 seconds. Drizzle again and turn one last time. Once the chicken is cooked and the glaze has caramelised, transfer to a board, cover with foil and leave to rest.

4. To make the risotto, heat the remaining 4 tablespoons of oil in a large, high-sided frying pan or heavy-based saucepan over a medium heat. Add the onion and fry for 5 minutes or until softened but not browned.

5. Add the rice and fry for 3 minutes, stirring constantly. Stir in the thyme and saffron. Pour in the wine and let it bubble and reduce by half. Add 1 ladleful of stock and bring to a simmer. Stir continuously until the liquid has been absorbed. Continue adding the rest of the stock in the same way, until the rice is cooked but still has a slight bite. This will take about 18 minutes.

6. Remove the pan from the heat. Add the butter and pecorino and stir for about 30 seconds. Season with salt and pepper. Slice the chicken. Divide the risotto between 4 bowls and place the chicken on top, together with some thyme sprigs.

Pasta, rice & gnocchi

Chestnut and Italian sausage risotto

Risotto con castagne e salsicce Italiane

Italians love their chestnuts and there are different varieties found throughout the country, including the rounder, fuller *marroni* and the smaller, flatter *castagne*. They are so versatile and can be roasted, boiled, puréed and candied, and added to soups, salads, pasta, risottos and desserts. They are also a popular street food; roasted chestnuts are sold from pushcarts in autumn and make a great snack. Here the chestnuts add depth and a sweet nuttiness, which complements the herby Italian sausages perfectly.

Serves 4

3 tablespoons olive oil
3 coarse, Italian-style sausages (about 200g), skins removed
1 onion, peeled and finely chopped
1 celery stick, finely chopped
2 tablespoons chopped fresh thyme, plus extra sprigs to garnish

300g Arborio or Carnaroli rice
6 tablespoons brandy
1.2 litres hot vegetable stock
100g cooked, peeled chestnuts (vacuum-packed), finely chopped
100g unsalted butter, cut into cubes
130g freshly grated Parmesan cheese
Freshly ground black pepper

1. Heat 1 tablespoon of oil in a large, high-sided frying pan or heavy-based saucepan over a medium heat. When hot, add the sausage meat. Break it up with a wooden spoon and fry for about 5 minutes or until browned. Transfer to a plate using a slotted spoon.

2. Heat the remaining 2 tablespoons of oil in the pan. Add the onion, celery and thyme and fry for 3–5 minutes or until softened but not browned. Return the sausage meat to the pan.

3. Add the rice and fry for about 3 minutes, stirring continuously, until the grains are coated and shiny.

4. Pour in the brandy and let it bubble for 1 minute or until it has evaporated.

5. Add 2 ladlesful of stock and bring to a simmer. Stir continuously until the liquid has been absorbed. Continue adding the rest of the stock in the same way. After 12–15 minutes, add the chestnuts. Continue to add the stock, cooking for a further 5 minutes or until the rice is cooked but still has a slight bite. You may not use all the stock.

6. Remove the pan from the heat and add the butter and Parmesan, stirring for about 30 seconds until creamy. Season with black pepper. Ladle into warm bowls and garnish with the thyme sprigs. Serve immediately.

Spinach and ricotta gnocchi in sage butter

Gnocchi di spinaci e ricotta con burro alla salvia

Gnocchi are Italian dumplings traditionally made from flour, egg and mashed potato. I sometimes find them a little bit heavy, so I have omitted the potato in this recipe. These gnocchi are lighter, but at the same time delicious and filling. If serving to vegetarians, replace the Parmesan with a rennet-free Italian hard cheese.

Serves 4

400g fresh spinach, thick stalks removed
150g ricotta cheese, drained
100g freshly grated Parmesan cheese, plus extra to serve
2 medium egg yolks
75g '00' grade pasta flour
½ teaspoon freshly grated nutmeg
60g unsalted butter
6 fresh sage leaves
Salt and freshly ground black pepper

1. Wash the spinach, place it in a large pan with some water still clinging to the leaves, cover and cook for 5 minutes or until tender. Drain thoroughly in a colander. Press on the spinach using the back of a wooden spoon to extract as much water as possible. When the spinach is cool enough to handle, squeeze it to extract any remaining water. Chop the spinach finely.

2. Put the spinach in a large bowl and add the ricotta, Parmesan, egg yolks, flour and nutmeg. Season with salt and pepper. Mix well to combine. Line two large baking sheets with baking parchment.

3. To form the gnocchi, scoop some of the mixture (about the size of a walnut) into a dessertspoon. Carefully transfer the mixture to another dessertspoon, turning and smoothing each side. Repeat the process several times until you have a neat, smooth egg shape with pointed ends. The mixture should make about 40 gnocchi. Lay the gnocchi on the lined baking sheets and chill for about 45 minutes to 1 hour.

4. Bring a large pan of salted water to the boil. Meanwhile, melt the butter in a large frying pan and add the sage. Leave on the lowest heat setting to keep warm.

5. Drop half the gnocchi into the water. Simmer gently for about 3 minutes. They are ready when they rise to the surface. Using a slotted spoon, remove a few at a time and transfer to the frying pan with the sage butter (between each spoonful, tap the spoon on kitchen paper to get rid of excess water). Repeat for the remaining gnocchi.

6. Once all the gnocchi are in the frying pan, increase the heat to medium and spoon the melted butter over the gnocchi to coat. Serve in warm bowls with freshly grated Parmesan and black pepper.

Pizza & breads

Making your own pizzas and bread is a great way to get creative. Try the delicious recipes in this chapter and then use your imagination to adapt them and invent your own variations.

Butternut squash, red onion, cavolo nero and Dolcelatte pizza with walnuts

Pizza con zucca violina, cipolla rossa, cavolo nero, Dolcelatte e noci

I wanted to try something different from a traditional pizza topping and I'm glad I did, as this pizza is delicious. The sweetness of the butternut squash works perfectly with the earthy cavolo nero, and the walnuts give added texture. When making this pizza for my vegan friends, I use a little tomato pizza sauce on the base and pile on all the other toppings minus the Dolcelatte. Serve with a green salad.

Makes 4

400g strong white flour, plus extra for dusting
2 x 7g sachets of fast-action (easy-blend) dried yeast
1½ teaspoons salt
4 tablespoons extra virgin olive oil, plus extra for greasing and brushing

For the topping
500g butternut squash, peeled and cut into 2cm cubes
2 red onions, peeled and cut into 8 wedges
8 tablespoons extra virgin olive oil, plus extra for greasing
2 tablespoons chopped fresh oregano
200g cavolo nero, tough central midribs removed and leaves cut across into quarters
1 garlic clove, peeled and thinly sliced
200g Dolcelatte cheese, cut into small pieces
60g walnut pieces
Salt and freshly ground black pepper

1. To make the dough, put the flour in a large bowl. Add the yeast to one side of the bowl and the salt to the other. Make a well in the centre and add the oil then gradually pour in 280ml of warm water.

2. Using the handle of a wooden spoon, mix together thoroughly to create a wet dough. Turn out the dough onto a well-floured surface and knead for about 5 minutes or until smooth and elastic.

3. Shape the dough into a round and place in a large oiled bowl. Brush the top with a little oil and cover with cling film. Leave to rest at room temperature for 20–25 minutes.

4. Brush 4 baking sheets with oil and set aside. Preheat the oven to 180°C/gas mark 4.

5. Meanwhile, make the topping. Place the butternut squash, onions, 3 tablespoons of the oil and half the oregano in a roasting tin, about 20 x 30cm. Season with salt and pepper. Mix together well with your hands, ensuring everything is evenly coated in the oil. Roast for 25 minutes then set aside. Increase the oven temperature to 220°C/gas mark 7.

$\longrightarrow$

6. Blanch the cavolo nero in a large saucepan of salted water for 5 minutes or until tender. Drain well and squeeze out any excess water.

7. Put the garlic in a medium saucepan or frying pan. Add 1 tablespoon of the oil and heat over a medium heat. Fry the garlic for 1 minute then add the cavolo nero, stirring to break it up. Season with salt and pepper. Set aside.

8. Turn out the dough onto a lightly floured surface and knead just 3 or 4 times to knock out the air. Quarter the dough and roll out each piece onto an oiled baking sheet, rolling and stretching the dough to make 4 rounds about 25cm in diameter and 1–2cm thick. Make a small rim by pulling up the edges slightly.

9. Divide the cavolo nero, butternut squash and onions equally over the surface of the pizza bases, avoiding the rim. Drizzle 1 tablespoon of oil over each pizza.

10. Bake for 12–14 minutes or until golden brown. Remove from the oven, scatter the Dolcelatte evenly over the vegetables, then sprinkle over the walnuts and remaining oregano. Return to the oven for 2 further minutes. Grind over some black pepper before serving.

Pizza topped with mushrooms and Taleggio

Pizza ai funghi e Taleggio

However much I adore a traditional pizza I sometimes crave the richness of something more than mozzarella. Taleggio, with its fruity tang and creamy qualities, turns an ordinary pizza into something quite decadent. Serve with a mixed salad.

Makes 4

400g strong white flour, plus extra for dusting

2 x 7g sachets of fast-action (easy-blend) dried yeast

1½ teaspoons salt

4 tablespoons extra virgin olive oil, plus extra for greasing

For the topping

400g passata

3 garlic cloves, peeled and 2 crushed, 1 thinly sliced

1 tablespoon chopped fresh oregano

50g unsalted butter

350g chestnut mushrooms, sliced

200g Taleggio cheese, rind removed and thinly sliced

4 tablespoons extra virgin olive oil

16 fresh basil leaves

Salt and freshly ground black pepper

1. First make the dough (see steps 1–3, page 141). Brush 4 baking sheets with oil and set aside. Preheat the oven to 220°C/gas mark 7.

2. Meanwhile, make the topping. Pour the passata into a medium saucepan and add the crushed garlic and oregano. Season with salt and pepper. Cook over a low to medium heat for 10 minutes or until the sauce starts to thicken. Set aside.

3. Melt the butter in a medium saucepan over a medium heat. Add the mushrooms and sliced garlic and season with salt and pepper. Fry for 4 minutes or until softened. Using a slotted spoon, transfer the mushrooms to a plate lined with kitchen paper. Set aside.

4. Turn out the dough onto a lightly floured surface and knead just 3 or 4 times to knock out the air. Quarter the dough and roll out each quarter directly onto an oiled baking sheet, rolling and stretching the dough to make 4 rounds about 25cm in diameter and 1–2cm thick. Make a small rim by pulling up the edges slightly.

5. Using the back of a tablespoon, spread the passata mixture evenly over the pizza bases, avoiding the rim. Scatter over the mushrooms and Taleggio. Drizzle 1 tablespoon of oil over each pizza.

6. Bake for 12–14 minutes or until golden brown. Remove from the oven, scatter over the basil and return to the oven for 1 further minute.

Pizza & breads

[143]

Mozzarella, anchovy, olive and sage pizza

Pizza con mozzarella, acciughe, olive e salvia

The Adriatic coast is not as well known for its pizza as some other regions in Italy, but you can still find great pizzerias. Like any true Neapolitan, I'm always on the lookout for great pizza and after a day's filming I enjoy nothing more than relaxing with a slice of pizza in one hand and a beer in the other. The pizza always has anchovies and the beer is always Italian.

Makes 4

400g strong white flour, plus extra for dusting

2 x 7g sachets of fast-action (easy-blend) dried yeast

1½ teaspoons salt

4 tablespoons extra virgin olive oil, plus extra for greasing and brushing

For the topping

400g passata

2 garlic cloves, peeled and crushed

1 tablespoon chopped fresh oregano

2 x 125g balls of mozzarella cheese, roughly chopped

20 anchovy fillets in oil, drained

40 pitted black olives, drained and halved

4 tablespoons extra virgin olive oil

20 small fresh sage leaves

Salt and freshly ground black pepper

1. First make the dough (see steps 1–3, page 141). Brush 4 baking sheets with oil and set aside. Preheat the oven to 220°C/gas mark 7.

2. Meanwhile, make the topping. Pour the passata into a medium saucepan and add the garlic and oregano. Season with salt and pepper. Cook over a low to medium heat for 10 minutes or until the sauce starts to thicken. Set aside.

3. Turn out the dough onto a lightly floured surface and knead just 3 or 4 times to knock out the air. Quarter the dough and roll out each quarter directly onto an oiled baking sheet, rolling and stretching the dough to make 4 rounds about 25cm in diameter and 1–2cm thick. Make a small rim by pulling up the edges slightly.

4. Using the back of a tablespoon, spread the passata mixture evenly over the pizza bases, avoiding the rim. Scatter over the mozzarella, anchovies and olives. Drizzle 1 tablespoon of oil over each pizza.

5. Bake for 12–14 minutes or until golden brown. Remove from the oven, scatter over the sage and return to the oven for 2 further minutes. Grind over some black pepper just before serving.

Grilled piadina with a courgette and Parmesan topping

Piadina con zucchine e Parmigiano fatta alla griglia

A piadina is an Italian version of a flatbread. A popular street food all over Emilia-Romagna, the piadina has been added to the Italian region's list of traditional food products. Piadine can be stuffed with meat, vegetables or cheeses, and I sampled them all with gusto when filming in Ravenna! Here I've added a courgette and Parmesan cheese topping after cooking the bread, but you can leave this stage out and fill the piadina as you would a wrap, or make a sandwich with ingredients of your choice (see page 151). You can also leave them plain and serve warm with soups or dips.

Makes 8
450g '00' grade Italian bread flour or strong white flour
2 teaspoons salt
3 teaspoons baking powder
1 tablespoon chopped fresh rosemary (optional)

4 tablespoons extra virgin olive oil
1 large courgette (about 250g)
25g freshly grated Parmesan cheese
Freshly ground black pepper

1. Combine the flour, salt, baking powder and rosemary, if using, in a medium bowl. Make a well in the centre and gradually add the oil and 240ml water. Mix together using the handle of a wooden spoon to form a soft dough.

2. Gather the dough and knead for 8–10 minutes or until smooth (there is no need to dust the work surface with flour).

3. Divide the dough into 8 equal-sized pieces and roll out each into a thin disc, about 25cm in diameter.

4. Heat a large frying pan over a medium to high heat. Add one of the piadine and cook for 2 minutes, then turn and cook for a further 2 minutes. Lay a sheet of greaseproof paper on the work surface. Transfer the piadina to the greaseproof paper and cover with a tea towel to keep warm. Repeat for all the piadine, laying a sheet of greaseproof paper between each one and covering the pile with the tea towel.

5. Preheat the grill to high. Meanwhile, using a vegetable peeler, shave the courgettes lengthways into long, thin strips.

6. Arrange several courgette slices on top of each piadina and sprinkle over the Parmesan. Transfer to the grill for 2 minutes (you will need to grill in batches). Season with black pepper and serve immediately.

Two piadina sandwiches with rough-and-ready pesto

Piadine farcite in due modi diversi con pesto semplice e veloce

I made these sandwiches for Rita at Ca' de Ven using her delicious bread fresh from the oven, but you can make your own piadine (see page 149). The pesto (which is used for both sandwiches) can be made with a food processor or in a pestle and mortar, but this method gives a rougher texture and more natural look. Use ordinary mozzarella if you can't find scamorza.

Makes 2
60g fresh basil
1 large garlic clove, peeled
60g pine nuts
100g freshly grated pecorino cheese
130ml extra virgin olive oil
2 piadina breads (see page 149)

For the chargrilled vegetable piadina
4 fine asparagus spears, woody ends trimmed
½ courgette, cut lengthways into long, thin slices

2 slices of aubergine (about 5mm thick)
3 tablespoons olive oil
3–4 tablespoons mayonnaise

For the ham and cheese piadina
4–6 slices of Italian cured meats (Parma ham, mortadella, Bresaola)
250g scamorza cheese (smoked mozzarella), rind removed and sliced
2 handfuls of rocket (about 40g)

1. First make the pesto. Finely chop the basil, garlic and pine nuts. Put in a medium bowl and add the pecorino. Gradually pour in the oil and stir well to mix. Set aside.

2. Chargrill the vegetables. Preheat a ridged cast-iron chargrill pan over a high heat for 5–10 minutes. Brush the asparagus, courgette and aubergine with the oil. Chargrill in batches for 5–10 minutes or until tender, turning halfway through cooking. Season with salt and pepper. Set aside.

3. Put the piadine in a dry frying pan and heat briefly over a medium heat then slice in half.

4. Assemble the chargrilled vegetable piadina. Put 4 tablespoons of the pesto and the mayonnaise in a bowl and mix well. Spread the mixture over one half of the piadina. Top with the chargrilled vegetables and drizzle over half the remaining pesto. Cover with the other half piadina and slice the sandwich in half.

5. Assemble the ham and cheese piadina. Spread the remaining pesto over one half of the piadina, then top with the rocket, scamorza and ham (use any combination of your favourite Italian cured meats in any quantities you like). Cover with the other half piadina and slice the sandwich in half.

Stromboli with Parma ham, mozzarella and fontina

Stromboli con prosciutto crudo, mozzarella e fontina

Stromboli are perfect for picnics or lunch boxes; they can be prepared ahead and they're pretty much a self-contained meal. Fontina is an excellent melting cheese, and I love its buttery nutty flavour. Here I've combined it with mozzarella and Parma ham, but any favourite filling of your choice can work well. Serve warm with a mixed salad, or leave to cool and wrap in foil ready to take on your picnic.

Serves 4

450g '00' grade Italian bread flour or strong white flour
1 x 7g sachet fast-action (easy-blend) dried yeast
1 teaspoon salt
3 tablespoons extra virgin olive oil, plus extra for greasing and brushing
120g sliced Parma ham

50g pitted black olives, drained
100g fresh mixed baby tomatoes, halved
1 x 125g ball of mozzarella cheese, finely chopped
150g fontina cheese, rind removed and cut into small cubes
8 fresh basil leaves
Freshly ground black pepper
2 large pinches of sea salt flakes

1. Combine the flour, yeast and salt in a large bowl. Make a well in the centre and pour in the oil and 300ml of hand-hot water. Mix together using the handle of a wooden spoon to form a soft dough. Gather the dough and knead for 8–10 minutes or until smooth and elastic (there is no need to dust the work surface with flour).

2. Shape the dough into a round and place in a large oiled bowl. Cover with cling film and leave in a warm place for about 1 hour or until doubled in size. Grease a large baking sheet with a little oil.

3. Tip the dough onto a lightly floured work surface. Roll into a rectangle measuring about 45 x 34cm.

4. Arrange the Parma ham on the dough, leaving a border of about 2cm all round. Scatter over the olives, tomatoes, mozzarella, fontina and basil. Season with pepper.

5. Starting from one of the shorter sides, roll up the dough, tucking the side edges under to seal. Transfer the roll, seam-side down, to the oiled baking sheet. Cover with a tea towel and leave for a further 30 minutes. Meanwhile, preheat the oven to 200°C/gas mark 6.

6. Using a skewer, prick several holes in the dough, right through to the baking sheet. Brush with oil and sprinkle over the sea salt flakes. Bake for 35 minutes or until golden brown.

Puglian dough rings

Taralli

Think of taralli as Puglia's answer to the pretzel. They're made from a simple dough, which can be sweet or savoury, shaped into a ring. Traditionally, locals dunk taralli into wine, and I snacked on many of these while enjoying a glass or two when filming in Ostuni. For this recipe I've divided the dough into three: one third is flavoured with ground black pepper, another with fennel seeds, and the final third is left plain (my kids love to dip them in Nutella!). Enjoy with a glass of chilled white wine.

Makes about 75
500g plain flour
1 teaspoon salt
150ml extra virgin olive oil

200ml dry white wine
½ teaspoon fennel seeds
½ teaspoon ground black pepper

1. Combine the flour and salt in a large bowl. Gradually add the olive oil and wine. Mix together using the handle of a wooden spoon to make a soft dough.

2. Gather the dough and knead for 5 minutes or until smooth (there is no need to dust the work surface with flour).

3. Divide the dough into 3 equal-sized pieces. Add the fennel seeds to one and the pepper to another, kneading each for a couple of minutes to distribute the spice evenly. Leave the third plain. Put the dough pieces on a large plate and cover with cling film. Chill for 15 minutes.

4. Meanwhile, preheat the oven to 200°C/gas mark 6. Line 2 large baking sheets with baking parchment and set aside.

5. To form the tarelli, take a small piece of dough (about the size of a walnut). Using the palms of your hands, roll out each piece to form a sausage shape about 10cm long and 4–5cm in diameter.

6. Bring the ends together to make a ring shape. Press the ends together to seal. Repeat until all the dough has been used up. Each third of dough should make about 25 taralli.

7. Bring a large saucepan of water to the boil. Plunge 6–10 dough rings at a time into the boiling water (try to separate them so they do not stick together) and cook for about 60 seconds or until they rise to the surface. Remove with a slotted spoon and transfer to a clean tea towel to dry. Repeat with the remaining dough rings.

8. Place the cooled dough rings on the lined baking trays. (They won't rise or spread so they can be placed quite close together.) Bake for 25 minutes or until golden.

Oregano, pancetta and potato bread

Pane con origano, pancetta e patate

There really is nothing like the smell of freshly baked bread, and this loaf is delicious served warm straight from the oven. I love adding potato to bread dough – it makes a really comforting loaf and, with the addition of pancetta, this bread is almost a meal in itself. It's perfect for dipping into a good-quality extra virgin olive oil.

Makes 1 loaf
200g Maris Piper potatoes, peeled and cut into chunks
375g strong white flour
1 x 7g sachet fast-action (easy-blend) dried yeast
¾ teaspoon salt

95g sliced pancetta, finely chopped
2 tablespoons chopped fresh oregano, plus 8–10 extra leaves to garnish
1 tablespoon extra virgin olive oil, plus extra for greasing and brushing
Large pinch of sea salt flakes
Freshly ground black pepper

1. Put the potatoes in a medium saucepan, cover with cold water and add some salt. Bring to the boil and simmer for 15–20 minutes or until tender. Drain and mash until really smooth. Transfer to a small bowl and press a piece of cling film on to the surface of the mashed potato to prevent it from drying out. Set aside to cool for 10 minutes.

2. Combine the flour, yeast and salt in a large bowl and season with black pepper. Using your fingers and thumbs, rub the mashed potato into the flour. Make a well in the centre and pour in 220ml of hand-hot water. Use the handle of a wooden spoon to mix to a soft dough. Beat the dough in the bowl for 5 minutes using the spoon.

3. Shape the dough into a round and place in a large oiled bowl. Cover with a damp tea towel and leave in a warm place for about 1 hour or until doubled in size.

4. Meanwhile, heat a small saucepan over a medium heat. Add the pancetta and fry for 5 minutes, stirring. Add the oregano and fry for 30 seconds. Set aside to cool slightly. Grease a loose-bottomed round cake tin, 24cm diameter.

5. Tip the contents of the pan into the dough. Return the dough to the floured work surface and knead for 5 minutes. Form the dough into a round and place in the greased tin. Cover lightly with a tea towel and leave to rise for a further 45 minutes or until doubled in size. Meanwhile, preheat the oven to 220°C/gas mark 7.

6. Brush oil over the reserved oregano leaves and place on the loaf. Drizzle over the oil and sprinkle over the sea salt flakes. Bake for 25 minutes or until golden. To test if the bread is cooked through, tap the bottom of the loaf; it should sound hollow. Transfer to a wire rack to cool slightly. Serve warm.

Polenta and pine nut bread

Pane con polenta e pinoli

For centuries, polenta was the staple food in the mountainous regions of Italy. Nowadays it is widely used and can be cooked in so many ways – baked as a main course, creamed or grilled as a side dish, and even sweetened as a dessert. In Veneto, polenta is so popular that it is often eaten for breakfast dipped in milk. Polenta is great for baking – it adds a rich texture to cakes, biscuits and breads. Here it adds an interesting crunchiness and, with the addition of pine nuts, gives a fantastic twist to a traditional loaf. Serve with some good-quality extra virgin olive oil and balsamic vinegar for dipping.

Makes 1 loaf
350g strong white flour
100g polenta, plus extra for the tin
1 x 7g sachet fast-action (easy-blend)
  dried yeast

1 teaspoon salt
1 teaspoon sugar
50g toasted pine nuts
2 tablespoons extra virgin olive oil, plus
  extra for greasing and brushing

1. Combine the flour, polenta, yeast, salt, sugar and pine nuts in a large bowl. Make a well in the centre and gradually pour in the oil and 275ml of hand-hot water. Mix together using the handle of a wooden spoon.

2. Gather the dough and knead for 8–10 minutes or until smooth and elastic (there is no need to dust the work surface with flour).

3. Shape the dough into a round and place in a large oiled bowl. Cover with cling film and leave in a warm place for about 1 hour or until doubled in size. Grease a large baking sheet with a little oil and sprinkle with polenta.

4. Knead the dough again for about 3 minutes. Form the dough into an oval measuring about 20 x 10cm and place on the prepared baking sheet. Cover loosely with a tea towel and leave to rise in a warm place for about 30 minutes or until doubled in size. Meanwhile, preheat the oven to 220°C/gas mark 7.

5. Make 6 deep diagonal cuts in the surface of the dough (3 per side). Bake for 25 minutes or until golden brown. If the bread browns too quickly, cover loosely with foil for the final 5 minutes of the cooking time to prevent burning. Transfer to a wire rack to cool. Serve warm or at room temperature.

Vegetables & sides

In Italy there are so many great vegetable dishes to choose from – they are often the star performer rather than simply a supporting player. Here are some of my favourites.

Baby courgette salad with chilli, basil, rocket and hazelnuts

Insalata di zucchine mignon con peperoncino, basilico, rucola e nocciole

In my opinion, baby courgettes are best eaten raw. Dressing them in garlic, balsamic vinegar, oil and herbs takes them to a whole new level. Always use good-quality extra virgin olive oil when dressing salads – it really does make a difference. Salads don't come easier than this, so do try it when courgettes are in season. Perfect as a side dish for your barbecue.

Serves 4–6

4 tablespoons balsamic vinegar, plus extra to drizzle
1 garlic clove, peeled and crushed
1 teaspoon runny honey
150ml extra virgin olive oil
1 fresh, medium-hot red chilli, deseeded and finely chopped
2 tablespoons shredded fresh basil
16 baby courgettes (about 400g in total)
30g roasted chopped hazelnuts
60g rocket leaves
Salt

1. Put the vinegar, garlic and honey in a medium bowl. Gradually add the oil and whisk until combined. Add the chilli and basil.

2. Using a vegetable peeler, shave the courgettes lengthways into long, thin strips. Add to the bowl and sprinkle over the hazelnuts. Season with salt and mix well.

3. Arrange the rocket on a large serving platter and pile the courgettes on top. Drizzle over a little vinegar (or balsamic glaze if you prefer). Serve immediately.

Mixed vegetable salad with almonds, olives and capers

Insalata mista di verdure con mandorle, olive e capperi

This is simple, tasty Italian cooking at its best. It's one of those dishes that has everyone 'ooing' when you bring it to the table because it looks so colourful and impressive. The salad can be prepared earlier in the day and just a drizzle of fresh olive oil will bring it back to life before serving.

Serves 4–6

50g blanched almonds

2 carrots, halved widthways and quartered lengthways

2 fennel bulbs, cored and cut into slices 1cm thick

4 celery sticks, cut into 3 widthways then halved lengthways

2 red peppers, deseeded and cut into 8 lengthways

400g baby courgettes, halved lengthways

Juice and zest of 1 unwaxed lemon

10 tablespoons extra virgin olive oil

30g capers, drained

100g pitted green olives, drained

Salt and freshly ground black pepper

1. Preheat the oven to 180°C/gas mark 4. Line a baking sheet with foil. Spread the almonds on the prepared baking sheet and toast in the oven for 10 minutes. Set aside.

2. Bring a large saucepan of salted water to the boil. Drop in the carrots and fennel and simmer for 5 minutes. Add the celery and peppers and simmer for 5 minutes. Finally, add the courgettes and simmer for 3 minutes. Drain thoroughly and set aside to cool.

3. Meanwhile, make the dressing. Put the lemon zest and juice in a small bowl. Gradually add 6 tablespoons of the oil and whisk to combine. Season with salt and pepper.

4. Once cool enough to handle, arrange the vegetables in block colours on a large serving platter. Scatter over the capers and olives. Drizzle over the dressing and scatter over the toasted almonds.

5. Drizzle over the remaining 4 tablespoons of oil and season with salt and pepper. Serve immediately.

Broccoli with wine, chillies, olives and pecorino

Broccoli con vino, peperoncino, olive e pecorino

Broccoli is a firm favourite in my house. It's such a versatile vegetable and I like to use it in soups, stews and pasta. Here, it is the star of the show – please don't overcook the broccoli as you will lose the texture. This recipe is based on one I tried when filming in the Tremiti Islands, a beautiful archipelago in the Adriatic Sea. It is a dish typical of the region – simple to cook, yet delicious. A perfect side dish for grilled meats or fish.

Serves 4
600–700g broccoli (about 2 heads), cut into
  small florets
3 tablespoons olive oil
2 fresh, medium-hot chillies, deseeded
  and finely chopped

50g pitted black olives, drained and
  roughly chopped
80ml dry white wine
50g freshly grated pecorino cheese
Salt

1. Bring a medium saucepan of salted water to the boil. Drop in the broccoli and simmer for 2 minutes. Drain thoroughly, rinse under cold running water and drain well again.

2. Heat the oil in a large frying pan over a medium to high heat. Add the drained broccoli, chillies and olives and fry for 1 minute. Add the wine and simmer for 5 minutes, stirring occasionally, until the broccoli is just tender.

3. Sprinkle over the pecorino, stir and cook for 1 minute. Serve immediately.

Fennel gratin

Finocchio gratinato

I find that many people don't quite know what to do with fennel, but it's such a versatile vegetable – it can be used raw in salads or stewed, pan-fried or baked. In this simple gratin, fennel is topped with breadcrumbs and Parmesan and baked until golden. I used small bulbs and halved them, but if you have larger bulbs cut them into slices 1cm thick after parboiling. Serve with roast chicken or simple grilled fish.

Serves 4–6

4 small fennel bulbs, cored and halved vertically
50g freshly grated Parmesan cheese
30g fresh white breadcrumbs
1 tablespoon chopped fresh thyme
50g unsalted butter, cut into small pieces, plus extra for greasing
Salt and freshly ground black pepper

1. Preheat the oven to 180°C/gas mark 4. Bring a large saucepan of salted water to the boil. Drop in the fennel and simmer for 5 minutes or until just tender. Drain and leave to cool slightly.

2. Combine the Parmesan, breadcrumbs and thyme in a small bowl.

3. Grease a baking dish, measuring about 30 x 20cm. Arrange the fennel on the bottom of the dish. Sprinkle over the breadcrumb mixture and season with salt and pepper.

4. Scatter the butter evenly over the breadrumbs. Bake for 20–25 minutes or until golden brown and bubbling.

Creamy spinach baked with mascarpone, ricotta and Parmesan

Spinaci cremosi al forno con mascarpone, ricotta e Parmigiano

It wasn't until I started making this dish that my kids would happily eat spinach. Italians have a serious relationship with spinach and other leafy greens, so I'm delighted that they have now seen the light! This tastes a little like creamed spinach, but the eggs make it lighter and fluffier. It's a perfect accompaniment to steak or roast chicken. When buying spinach, look for fresh dark green leaves with a crisp texture; avoid wilted or bruised leaves.

Serves 4–6

1kg fresh spinach, thick stalks removed
3 medium eggs
100g freshly grated Parmesan cheese
100g mascarpone cheese
100g ricotta cheese
¼ teaspoon freshly grated nutmeg
Salt and freshly ground black pepper

1. Preheat the oven to 180°C/gas mark 4. Wash the spinach, place it in a large pan with some water still clinging to the leaves, cover and cook for 5 minutes or until tender. Drain thoroughly in a colander. You may have to cook the spinach in 2 batches.

2. Press on the spinach using the back of a wooden spoon to extract as much water as possible. When the spinach is cool enough to handle, squeeze it to extract any remaining water. Roughly chop the spinach.

3. Break the eggs into a large bowl and beat together with the Parmesan, mascarpone, ricotta and nutmeg. Season well. Add the spinach and stir to combine.

4. Tip the mixture into a baking dish, about 25 x 20cm, and bake for 15 minutes. Serve immediately.

Puréed potato and celeriac with garlic, mascarpone and chives

Purè di patate e sedano rapa con aglio, mascarpone ed erba cipollina

Celeriac has a mild, slightly nutty celery flavour and, when cooked, a texture rather like a potato. What it lacks in appearance it most certainly makes up for in taste. Just be aware that it discolours quickly so, once sliced, immerse the pieces in a bowl of cold water. This creamy dish is perfect served with roast meat or baked or grilled fish. It can also be prepared ahead – simply cover with foil and reheat in the oven for about 30 minutes.

Serves 4
400g King Edward potatoes, peeled and cut into 2.5cm cubes
500g celeriac, peeled and cut into 2cm cubes

2 garlic cloves, peeled
35g unsalted butter
100g mascarpone cheese
2 tablespoons snipped fresh chives
Salt and freshly ground black pepper

1. Place the potatoes in one medium saucepan and the celeriac in another. Cover both with cold water, add some salt and drop a garlic clove into each pan. Bring to the boil then reduce the heat and simmer for 15–20 minutes or until tender. Drain both into the same colander.

2. Put the butter and mascarpone into one of the used pans. Place over a low heat for 2 minutes until melted. Remove from the heat and set aside.

3. Tip the drained potatoes and celeriac into a bowl and purée using a stick blender. Season well with salt and pepper.

4. Pour in the melted butter and mascarpone mixture. Blend again until smooth. Stir through three quarters of the chives and sprinkle the remaining chives on top. Serve immediately.

Potato and herb fritters

Frittelle di patate ed erbe

These are great as an antipasto, for a light lunch or brunch, or as a tasty side dish for grilled fish. Fritters of all kinds are so popular in Italy and although they're not the healthiest of foods they're certainly one of the tastiest! I shallow fry these fritters in olive oil so the naughtiness is kept to a minimum; you can therefore enjoy them without too much guilt!

Serves 4–6
800g Maris Piper potatoes, peeled
30g plain flour
3 tablespoons snipped fresh chives
1 tablespoon chopped fresh oregano
3 tablespoons chopped fresh flat-leaf parsley

2 eggs, lightly beaten
100g mascarpone cheese, plus extra to serve
1 tablespoon chopped fresh dill, plus extra sprigs to garnish
6 tablespoons olive oil
Salt and freshly ground black pepper

1. Grate the potatoes on the coarse side of a grater. Put them in a clean tea towel and squeeze out the excess water. Tip into a large bowl.

2. Add the flour, herbs and beaten egg. Stir until all the ingredients are thoroughly combined. Season with salt and pepper. Preheat the oven to 160°C/gas mark 3.

3. Put the mascarpone and dill in a small bowl and stir to combine. Season to taste.

4. Heat 2 tablespoons of the oil in a large frying pan over a medium to high heat. Spoon the mixture into the hot oil, 1 heaped tablespoon at a time. Press lightly with a fish slice and fry without moving for about 4 minutes each side or until golden. Transfer to a baking sheet and keep warm in the oven. Fry the rest in 2 batches, adding 2 tablespoons of oil to the pan before frying each new batch.

5. To serve, spoon a little mascarpone onto each fritter and place a sprig of dill on top.

Portobello mushrooms with pistachio and herb butter

Funghi Portobello con pistacchio e burro alle erbe

Italians eat a lot of mushrooms. Not only do they taste great, but they are also incredibly nutritious and are a good source of selenium, iron and vitamins B and D. Portobello mushrooms are ideal for stuffing – they are large and have a firm, meaty texture. This is one of those dishes where mushroom-haters become converted. Serve with a crisp green salad and bread or as an accompaniment to grilled fish.

Serves 4
1 tablespoon olive oil, plus extra for greasing
1 onion, peeled and finely chopped
4 Portobello mushrooms (about 275g in total), stalks removed and finely chopped
100g unsalted butter (room temperature)
50g shelled pistachios, finely chopped

Grated zest of 1 unwaxed lemon and juice of ½ lemon
1 garlic clove, peeled and finely chopped
3 tablespoons finely chopped fresh flat-leaf parsley, plus extra leaves to garnish
1 tablespoon finely chopped fresh thyme
1 tablespoon finely chopped fresh oregano
Salt and freshly ground black pepper

1. Preheat the oven to 180°C/gas mark 4. Grease a baking dish large enough to hold the mushrooms snugly, about 22 x 22cm.

2. Heat the oil in a small saucepan over a medium heat. Add the onion and fry for 3 minutes. Stir in the mushroom stalks and fry for 2 minutes or until softened. Remove from the heat and set aside.

3. Put the butter in a small bowl and add the pistachios, lemon zest and juice, garlic and herbs. Mix thoroughly to combine. Season well with salt and pepper.

4. Put the mushrooms in the greased dish, cup-side up. Spoon the onion mixture into the mushroom cups. Spread the pistachio butter on top.

5. Bake for 20 minutes. Sprinkle with some parsley and serve immediately.

Spicy roasted aubergines

Melanzane piccanti al forno

Although grown and treated as a vegetable, the aubergine is in fact a fruit, as it bears seeds within its flesh. When an aubergine is cooked correctly it's simply delicious and happily soaks up any flavour you pair with it. This dish, in which the aubergine is the star, can be served as a meat-free main course or as a side dish; it's particularly good with lamb. Make sure you brush the aubergine with the oil rather than pouring it over. If poured, the oil simply sinks into the flesh, giving you overly oily patches. Serve with a mixed salad.

Serves 8 as a side, 4 as a main course
4 aubergines, halved lengthways
6 tablespoons extra virgin olive oil, plus extra for greasing
2 fresh, medium-hot red chillies, deseeded and finely sliced

75g toasted pine nuts
3 tablespoons shredded fresh basil
1 tablespoon runny honey
1 garlic clove, peeled and crushed
50g freshly grated Parmesan cheese
Salt

1. Preheat the oven to 200°C/gas mark 6. Grease a large shallow roasting tin.

2. Place the aubergines cut-side up in the roasting tin. Brush with 2 tablespoons of the oil. Sprinkle over the chillies and season with salt. Bake for 25 minutes.

3. Meanwhile, put the pine nuts, basil, honey, garlic, Parmesan and remaining 4 tablespoons of the oil in a small bowl. Stir to combine.

4. Remove the aubergines from the oven and spoon the pine nut mixture evenly over the top of each aubergine. Return to the oven for 5 minutes then serve.

Aubergine and caciocavallo cheese bake

Parmigiana di melanzane al forno con caciocavallo

When we were filming in the Gargano National Park, in Puglia, I made this dish for Giuseppe Bramante and his family. I used their farm-made caciocavallo cheese produced with fresh Podolica cow's milk. Caciocavallo is a delicious stretched-curd cheese produced throughout southern Italy, but it is a particular delicacy in the Gargano peninsula. If you can't find caciocavallo cheese, use mozzarella. Serve with bread and a green salad.

Serves 6

5 large aubergines, cut lengthways into slices 1cm thick
4 tablespoons extra virgin olive oil
4 x 400g tins of chopped tomatoes
25g fresh basil leaves, torn, plus 10–20 whole leaves

150ml olive oil
150ml sunflower oil
12 eggs, lightly beaten
375g caciocavallo cheese, torn into pieces
100g freshly grated pecorino
Salt and freshly ground pepper

1. Sprinkle some salt over the aubergines and place on a draining rack or in a colander set over the sink for about 2 hours.

2. Meanwhile, heat the extra virgin olive oil in a medium saucepan over a medium heat. Add the tomatoes and the whole basil leaves. Season with salt and pepper. Simmer gently for 15 minutes. Remove from the heat and set aside.

3. Pat the aubergines with kitchen paper to remove any excess liquid. Heat the olive oil and sunflower oil together in a large non-stick frying pan over a medium heat.

4. Dip 3–4 slices of aubergine (or as many slices as will fit in your pan in a single layer) into the beaten egg then carefully lay the slices in the hot

oil. Fry for 2–3 minutes each side or until golden and cooked through. Lift out with a fish slice and transfer to kitchen paper to drain. Repeat with the remaining aubergine slices, frying in batches. Add more oil between batches if necessary.

5. Preheat the oven to 170°C/gas mark 3. Lay a layer of aubergine slices in the bottom of a baking dish, about 34 x 24cm (a little overlap is fine). Spread a quarter of the tomato sauce over the aubergines. Scatter over a quarter of the caciocavallo cheese then a quarter of the torn basil leaves and quarter of the pecorino. Repeat the process 3 more times.

6. Bake for 20 minutes or until golden and bubbling around the edges.

Desserts

We Italians have a bit of a sweet tooth. We love our ice cream, of course, and all kinds of pastries and biscuits. We don't overdo it – just a taste here and a nibble there – but there's no doubt that we absolutely adore something sweet.

Fresh mint and chocolate chip ice cream

Gelato con gocce di cioccolato e menta fresca

When I was a child I always gravitated towards mint choc chip. Now when I taste this flavour I am often disappointed by the artificial toothpaste-like flavour of the mint. I wanted to make a fresh-tasting ice cream that reminded me of my childhood, so the colours and flavours in this recipe are completely natural. Only use the leaves of the mint. The ice cream will become very fibrous if the stalks are used and the colour won't be such a vivid green.

Serves 4–6
50g fresh mint leaves
4 medium egg yolks
100g caster sugar
1 teaspoon cornflour

200ml double cream
400ml full-fat milk
100g good-quality, plain dark chocolate, finely chopped, plus extra for sprinkling
Mint sprigs to decorate

1. Bring a small saucepan of water to the boil. Add the mint leaves and boil for 60 seconds. Drain and plunge the leaves into ice-cold water for a few minutes, then drain again. Pat dry with kitchen paper. Set aside.

2. Make a rich custard. Put the egg yolks and sugar in a large heatproof bowl and whisk for 2 minutes with an electric whisk until thick and pale. Add the cornflour and whisk to combine.

3. Pour the double cream and milk into a medium saucepan and gently heat until just below boiling point. Gradually whisk the hot cream and milk into the egg mixture. Pour the mixture back into the saucepan through a sieve (rinse out the pan first or the mixture can burn).

4. Remove 2 ladlesful of the custard and put in a food processor or blender with the blanched mint leaves. Blitz until the mint is very finely chopped and the mixture is bright green. Pour the mixture back into the saucepan with the rest of the custard.

5. Set the pan over a low heat and heat gently for 10 minutes, stirring constantly, until the custard is thick enough to coat the back of spoon. Do not boil, or the eggs will curdle.

6. Pour the custard into a shallow 3-litre rigid freezerproof container and leave to cool for at least 1 hour. Transfer to the fridge for at least 2 hours to chill.

7. Place the container in the freezer for 1 hour. Remove from the freezer and whisk the mixture. Return to the freezer for 1 further hour then whisk again. Repeat once more then during the final whisk add the chocolate. At this stage, the ice cream can be either left in the freezerproof container or transferred to a glass serving bowl. Return to the freezer for 1–2 hours until firm.

8. About 10 minutes before serving, remove from the freezer. Decorate with mint sprigs and sprinkle over the extra chocolate.

Almond tiramisù with cherry and amaretto compote

Tiramisù con mandorle e composta di ciliegie al liquore d'amaretto

Literally meaning 'pick me up', tiramisù is probably the best known dessert from my home country and everyone has their own twist on the traditional. I like to use amaretto, and here I've paired the dessert with a delicious cherry compote. The tiramisù can be made a day ahead if you prefer.

Serves 8
200ml strong espresso coffee (cold)
200ml amaretto (almond liqueur)
200ml double cream
5 medium eggs, separated
6 tablespoons caster sugar
500g mascarpone cheese
275g Savoiardi biscuits (sponge fingers)

½ tablespoon cocoa powder for dusting
80g toasted flaked almonds

For the compote
400g pitted cherries
75ml amaretto (almond liqueur)
2 tablespoons caster sugar

1. Pour the coffee into a bowl and stir in 100ml of the amaretto. Set aside. Pour the cream into a bowl and whip until thick enough to hold its shape and form soft peaks. Set aside. Put the egg whites in a bowl and whisk with an electric whisk on full speed until they form stiff peaks.

2. Tip the egg yolks into a large bowl and add the sugar. Whisk with a balloon whisk for about 5 minutes or until thick and pale and increased in volume. Add the mascarpone and whisk to combine. Gently fold in the whipped cream and remaining 100ml of amaretto.

3. Using a metal spoon, gently fold one third of the egg whites into the mascarpone mixture until well blended. Fold in the remaining egg whites until well combined. Set aside.

4. Dip one of the biscuits in the coffee and amaretto mixture for no more than two seconds.

Lay the biscuit, sugar-side up, in the base of a ceramic dish, about 23 x 23 x 9cm. Repeat the process, lining up the biscuits, until the bottom of the dish is covered.

5. Spread half the mascarpone mixture over the biscuits, then cover with another layer of the remaining biscuits dipped in coffee as previously. To finish, top with the remaining mascarpone mixture and smooth the surface. Loosely cover with cling film and chill for at least 4 hours.

6. Meanwhile, make the compote. Put the cherries in a small pan with the amaretto and sugar. Bring to the boil. Simmer for 1 minute then leave to cool.

7. Just before serving, carefully remove the cling film, dust the top of the tiramisù with a thick layer of cocoa powder and sprinkle over the almonds. Serve with the cherry compote.

Honey figs with cinnamon-sugared almonds

Fichi al miele con mandorle pralinate alla cannella

Figs are a real Italian favourite and I love using them in desserts. Exploding with flavour, the jammy sweetness of the cooked figs goes beautifully with the creamy mascarpone and crunchy almonds. I've doubled the quantity of cinnamon-sugared almonds needed here purely because I know that once you've tasted them you'll find it difficult to leave any to scatter over the figs!

Serves 4

25g icing sugar
1¼ teaspoons ground cinnamon
100g blanched almonds
25g unsalted butter

3 tablespoons runny honey
8 ripe figs (about 250g in total), halved
  vertically
100g mascarpone cheese

1. Preheat the oven to 180°C/gas mark 4. Line a baking sheet with baking parchment and set aside.

2. Put the icing sugar and 1 teaspoon of the cinnamon in a small bowl. Add 1½ teaspoons of water and stir to form a paste. Tip in the almonds and mix well until all are evenly coated in the paste.

3. Tip the coated almonds onto the lined baking sheet in a single layer. Bake for 10 minutes. Remove from the oven and leave to cool. Once the almonds are cool enough to handle, separate any that are stuck together and set aside.

4. Melt the butter in a medium frying pan over a medium heat. Stir in 2 tablespoons of the honey. Place the figs in the pan, cut-side down, and cook for 4–5 minutes.

5. Meanwhile, put the mascarpone, remaining 1 tablespoon of honey and remaining ¼ teaspoon of cinnamon in a small bowl. Stir to combine.

6. To serve, arrange 4 fig halves on each plate. Place a spoonful of the mascarpone mixture alongside the figs. Drizzle the sauce from the pan evenly over and around the figs and mascarpone. Scatter over the sugared almonds.

Chocolate-coated fruit with cheeky toppings

Frutta ricoperta di cioccolato e guarnizioni ai sapori audaci

This dish really is all about using your imagination and just going for it; there are no rules. It's a sweet treat that's easy and fun to prepare – and I'm guessing that it can't be too bad for you if there's fruit involved! The crew loved these chocolate-covered fruits and I hope you do too. The best way to approach the dipping stage is to have all your ingredients out in front of you and then just play around with combinations of fruit and chocolate.

Serves 4

150g good-quality plain dark chocolate
150g good-quality white chocolate
Assortment of prepared fruit (about 800g in total), e.g. peaches (halved and stone removed), strawberries, mango (peeled and cut lengthways into large chunks), dried figs and fresh coconut chunks

For the toppings

1 tablespoon chopped fresh mint
1 tablespoon pink peppercorns, roughly crushed
1 tablespoon dried chilli flakes
1 tablespoon finely chopped hazelnuts
4 amaretti biscuits, crushed

1. Melt both types of chocolate separately. Break the chocolate into a heatproof bowl. Place the bowl over a saucepan of gently simmering water and heat gently until just melted (do not stir) then remove the pan from the heat and stir. Alternatively, heat the chocolate for 20 seconds in the microwave (medium for white chocolate, high for dark chocolate), then remove and stir. Return to the microwave and repeat until most of the pieces have melted, then remove and let the remaining chocolate melt in the residual heat. Leave to cool for 3–5 minutes.

2. Line a tray with baking parchment. Dip the fruit into the melted chocolate and lay it on the prepared tray. Sprinkle with your chosen toppings immediately.

Here are some of my favourite toppings:

• Peaches dipped one side in white chocolate and sprinkled with mint and pink peppercorns
• Strawberries with dark chocolate and amaretti biscuits; strawberries with white chocolate and hazelnuts
• Mango with dark chocolate and amaretti biscuits; mango with white chocolate, pink peppercorns and mint
• Coconut with dark chocolate, chilli and amaretti biscuits
• Dried figs in dark chocolate with amaretti biscuits and chilli

3. Leave to set for at least 1 hour or chill for 30 minutes before serving.

Cherry and amaretto tart

Crostata alle ciliegie e liquore d'amaretto

Cherry and amaretto is a match made in heaven – this delicious tart is all the proof you need. The hardest part of this recipe is transferring the pastry into the tart case. I find that rolling the pastry directly onto floured cling film helps. Simply roll the pastry around the rolling pin with the cling film in place and roll it over the case with the cling film facing upwards, and then peel off the film. Serve with fresh cream, mascarpone or vanilla ice cream.

Serves 8
225g plain white flour
160g unsalted butter (chilled), diced
65g icing sugar, plus extra for dusting
Pinch of salt
2 medium egg yolks

For the filling
100g icing sugar
100g ground almonds
2 medium eggs, lightly beaten
½ teaspoon almond essence
2 tablespoons amaretto (almond liqueur)
450g ripe cherries, pitted

1. First make the pastry. Put the flour, butter, icing sugar and salt in a food processor. Blitz until the mixture resembles fine breadcrumbs. Add the egg yolks and pulse very briefly for about 10 seconds. Tip the mixture into a bowl and gather into a ball with your hands. Cover and transfer to the fridge for 30 minutes.

2. Roll out the pastry onto floured cling film and use it to line a loose-bottomed, round tart tin (ideally fluted), 24cm in diameter. Trim the pastry. Chill for a further 15 minutes. Preheat the oven to 200°C/gas mark 6.

3. 'Blind bake' the pastry case. Prick the pastry base all over with a fork, line the bottom and sides with baking parchment and weigh it down with baking beans or rice. Place the tin on a baking sheet and bake for 12 minutes. Remove the beans or rice and paper, reduce the oven temperature to 170°C/gas mark 3 and cook for a further 5 minutes or until golden brown. Set aside to cool.

4. Meanwhile, make the filling. Combine the icing sugar, almonds, beaten eggs, almond essence and amaretto in a bowl. Tip the mixture into the pastry case. Arrange the cherries on top, pushing them lightly into the mixture.

5. Bake for 50 minutes or until the top is golden brown and firm to the touch. After 20 minutes, cover the edges with foil to prevent the edges from burning.

6. Leave to cool in the tin then place on a serving plate or board and dust with icing sugar.

Peach and mascarpone pastries with pistachios

Crostatine di pasta sfoglia con pesche, mascarpone e pistacchio

The region of Emilia-Romagna produces some of the most delicious peaches and nectarines that I've ever tasted. The optimal climate results in a sweet, juicy, scented flesh and the local farmers work hard to preserve the quality of this local favourite. You will find peach desserts all over Italy and this dish really lets the fruit shine.

Serves 4

320g shop-bought, ready-rolled, all-butter puff pastry
1 medium egg, lightly beaten
20g icing sugar, plus extra for dusting
250g mascarpone cheese

4 tablespoons single cream
1 vanilla pod, split lengthways and seeds scraped out
15g shelled pistachios, roughly chopped
2 ripe peaches, halved and thinly sliced
4 mint sprigs to decorate

1. Preheat the oven to 200°C/gas mark 6. Line a large baking sheet with baking parchment and set aside.

2. Unroll the pastry and cut in half lengthways, then in quarters across, to give 8 rectangles measuring about 12 x 9cm. Cut the centre out of 4 of the rectangles, leaving 1cm-wide frames. Brush the 4 complete rectangles with the beaten egg and place on the prepared baking sheet. Place a pastry frame on top of each complete rectangle and brush the frame tops with egg.

3. Prick the pastry bases with a fork several times and dust 1 teaspoon of the icing sugar over the cases. Bake for 15 minutes or until golden. Remove from the oven and leave to cool.

4. Put the remaining icing sugar, mascarpone, cream and vanilla seeds in a medium bowl. Tip in the pistachios and mix well.

5. Using the back of a teaspoon, press the centre of each rectangle in the pastry cases downwards to flatten slightly. Spread a layer of the mascarpone mixture on the base and arrange the peach slices on the mascarpone.

6. To serve, decorate with a mint sprig and dust over some extra icing sugar.

Custard tartlets

Pasticciotti

The beautiful town of Lecce, in Puglia, is known for its Baroque architecture, abundance of cherubs and gargoyles and, most importantly, its wonderful pasticciotti. These small pastries, with their flaky crust and creamy custard filling, are associated with this region of Italy as much as tea is associated with England. It's the breakfast of choice for the locals, but a pasticciotto can be enjoyed at any time of day, ideally served with a good cup of coffee.

Makes 10

250g plain white flour, plus extra for dusting
125g caster sugar
125g unsalted butter (chilled)
1 teaspoon baking powder
Pinch of salt
3 medium egg yolks
2 tablespoons full-fat milk (chilled), plus extra for brushing

Butter for greasing
1 medium egg, lightly beaten

For the filling
4 medium egg yolks
150g caster sugar
40g cornflour
500g full-fat milk
1 vanilla pod

1. First make the pastry. Put the flour, sugar, butter, baking powder and salt in a food processor and pulse until the mixture resembles fine breadcrumbs. Add the egg yolks and pulse for about 10 seconds, then the milk and pulse for 5 seconds.

2. Tip the mixture into a medium bowl and shape into a round. Wrap the pastry in cling film and transfer to the fridge for at least 30 minutes.

3. Meanwhile, make the custard filling. Put the egg yolks and sugar in a large heatproof bowl. Whisk for about 1 minute with an electric whisk until thick and pale. Whisk in the cornflour.

4. Put the milk in a medium saucepan. Split the vanilla pod in half lengthways and scrape out the seeds into the milk, then drop in the pod. Heat gently over a low to medium heat, stirring occasionally, until just below boiling point. Remove from the heat and set aside to cool slightly for about 2 minutes. Discard the vanilla pod.

5. Gradually pour the hot milk into the egg yolk mixture in a steady stream, whisking all the time. Strain the custard back into the pan (rinse the pan out first so the mixture doesn't burn). Heat gently over a low heat, whisking constantly for about 10 minutes or until thick and velvety. Do not boil, or the eggs will curdle. Pour the mixture into a heatproof bowl and lay cling film directly on the surface of the custard, to stop it forming a skin. Leave to cool completely, then chill in the fridge.

6. Preheat the oven to 180°C/gas mark 4. Lightly grease 10 holes in a muffin tray with butter. Cut off two thirds of the pastry, roll it out onto a lightly floured surface and use a 98mm biscuit cutter to make 10 discs. Line each hole of the muffin tray with a pastry disc.

7. Remove the cling film from the custard and divide the mixture among the pastry cases.

8. Roll out the remaining pastry and make 10 discs for the lids using a 78mm biscuit cutter.

9. Brush the rim of each pastry lining with a little milk, lay a pastry disc on top and press the edges down to seal. Brush the lids with the beaten egg. Bake for 15 minutes.

10. Allow the pastries to cool in the tin. Just before serving, run a knife around the holes and transfer the pastries to a serving platter.

Venetian doughnuts

Fritole Veneziane

Venetian doughnuts are simply delicious. Traditionally flavoured with citrus peel, raisins and pine nuts, they are made and sold by street vendors during the *Carnevale di Venezia* as a prelude to the beginning of Lent. The doughnuts are best enjoyed on the day they are made. Be very careful when deep-frying them – you don't want splashes and burns from the hot oil.

Makes about 40
125g raisins
120ml grappa
600g plain flour
2 x 7g sachets fast-action (easy-blend)
  dried yeast
Zest from 1 unwaxed lemon
200g caster sugar

Large pinch of salt
2 medium eggs, lightly beaten
50g toasted pine nuts
75g Italian mixed peel
250ml full-fat milk (lukewarm)
2 litres sunflower oil for deep-frying
1 teaspoon ground cinnamon

1. Put the raisins in a small bowl or cup, pour over the grappa and leave to soak for 20 minutes.

2. Meanwhile, combine the flour, yeast, lemon zest, 100g of the sugar and the salt in a large bowl. Make a well in the centre and stir in the beaten eggs. Add the pine nuts, mixed peel, soaked raisins and grappa and stir again. Pour in the milk. Mix together to form a sticky dough.

3. Cover the dough with a tea towel and leave to rise in a warm place for 1½ hours or until doubled in size.

4. Heat a deep-fat fryer to 180°C, or heat the oil in a deep pan or wok over a medium heat until very hot. To test the temperature, add a small piece of bread; it will sizzle when the oil is hot enough for frying.

5. Scoop some of the dough (about the size of a large walnut) into a dessertspoon. Carefully transfer it to another dessertspoon, turning and smoothing each side. Repeat the process several times to make a round.

6. Very carefully, slip the dough into the hot oil (you can make about 7–8 doughnuts at a time). Fry for 5 minutes, turning with a slotted spoon to ensure even browning on all sides. Remove with a slotted spoon and drain on kitchen paper. Fry the remaining doughnuts in batches. Leave to cool.

7. Combine the remaining 100g of sugar and the cinnamon in a small bowl. Roll the doughnuts in the cinnamon sugar and serve.

Panettone and honey pudding with chargrilled fruits and ricotta

Dolce di panettone e miele con frutta grigliata e ricotta

This is my Italian version of bread and butter pudding, served with chargrilled fruits and sweetened ricotta cheese. In Italy the ricotta is very creamy and rich, and I just added honey to sweeten it, but in Britain you might like to add a few drops of vanilla extract to give depth of flavour.

Serves 6

4 tablespoons runny honey, plus extra for drizzling
1 large panettone, cut into slices about 2.5cm thick
4 medium eggs
4 medium egg yolks
80g caster sugar
3 teaspoons vanilla extract
3 tablespoons Marsala wine
125ml double cream
500ml full-fat milk
30g Demerara sugar
½ trimmed pineapple, cut into large chunks
3 peaches, halved and stones removed
300g cherries, pitted
250g ricotta cheese
Few drops of vanilla extract (optional)
Icing sugar, for dusting

1. Preheat the oven to 160°C/gas mark 3. Lightly drizzle the honey over both sides of the panettone. Arrange the slices in a baking dish or shallow casserole, about 26 x 26cm.

2. Place the eggs, egg yolks, caster sugar, vanilla and Marsala in a large bowl. Whisk using a balloon whisk until pale. Gently whisk in the double cream and milk.

3. Pour the egg mixture over the panettone, pushing it down to soak up as much liquid as possible. Sprinkle over the Demerara sugar. Bake for 20 minutes or until the top is lightly browned and the custard is just set.

4. Meanwhile, preheat a cast-iron chargrill pan over a high heat for 5–10 minutes. Once hot, lay the pineapple and peaches in the pan and cook

for about 1–2 minutes each side (depending on the ripeness of the fruit) or until just softened and with chargrill markings. Remove the pan from the heat and toss in the cherries, leaving them to warm through in the residual heat.

5. Put the ricotta, honey and a few drops of vanilla extract (if using) in a medium bowl and stir to combine.

6. Serve the pudding with a large spoonful of the sweetened ricotta and chargrilled fruit and a dusting of icing sugar. Drizzle with a little extra honey.

Index

Author's note

Thank you again to my publisher, Nicky Ross, and to all at Hodder for their hard work and continued support. To Polly Boyd – you are just brilliant! To Alison Shalson for all of your work on the recipes and Lizzie Harris, Rob Allison, Georgia Vaux and Dan Jones for making the food and book look amazing. A very special thank you to my agents, Jeremy Hicks and Charlotte Leaper, for everything you do.

Thank you also to my great TV team for all of their *fantastico* work on the series – you guys are the best!

Gino xxx

The TV crew, from left to right:
Steve Horwood, sound recordist; Abbi-Rose Crook, make-up artist; Lilly Marchesi, assistant producer; Emily Burndred, producer; Rupert Binsley, director of photography; Gino; Ruth Binsley, series director; Rob Allison, home economist; Trevor Butterfield, second camera; Holly Bryson, assistant producer; Joseph Gray, runner; Paul Parisi, location facilitator